A Memoir of the Sixties
and Seventies in Greece

MY GREEK ODYSSEY

GEORGE B. SALIMBENE

DEDICATION

Liz and Theo my Koumbari who were there from the beginning
Sebastian and Marianne who always make my return a homecoming
Fanis and Cathy my Koumbari who were and are always there for me
Adrienne good colleague and valued friend
Dave my companion on the Mt. Athos trip and friend of many years
Demos and Voula who always open their arms and home
Chip and Aliki who braved the forest fire with us
Janey and Dimitri who always love an adventure
Jane and Alessia my companions on our American odyssey

CONTENTS

THE VOYAGE BEGINS

IN 1965 I WENT TO GREECE ON A FULBRIGHT GRANT. Selected to teach English as a Foreign Language to Greek University students in Athens, my wife, Suzanne, and I traveled to Greece on the Greek Liner Queen Frederika. When we stepped aboard to the strains of 'Never on Sunday' I sensed we were setting out on a great and much anticipated adventure, unaware that half a lifetime would pass before I would return to the United States.

The start of this journey began, in a sense, when I was quite young. At bedtime my mother would recount stories about her life in Brazil and the voyage she took as a young girl with her family from Sao Paolo, Brazil to New York City. Her parents were Italian immigrants who had first immigrated to Argentina and then moved to Brazil, where my mother was born.

She spoke of the ship, S.S. Vassari, anchoring in numerous ports to take on cargo of exotic fruits, timber and travelers from the different countries. She described colorfully dressed native women and the bands that raucously serenaded the ship at dockside. Children would dive into the harbors to fetch coins the passengers threw to them. Small boats would come alongside to sell fruit and souvenirs, exotic birds and monkeys in cages that were proffered for a few cents.

The second occurrence which fostered a deep desire for travel came as a youngster, when my uncles all returned safely from the Second World War. They told stories of the far off places that they had visited: the Pacific islands, Japan, Hawaii, Europe, and the strange customs and sights that they encountered. The ones who had been in combat, seldom spoke of their experiences in front of the children, only late at night when we were in bed, we could hear them talk about what they had experienced. For the children, the uncles dwelt on the strenuous rigors of basic training and tyrannical sergeants, who did everything possible to make their lives a misery, while turning the young recruits into soldiers. To me, it was all high adventure that I wanted to experience. Inevitably, while in high school and college, Hemingway became my favorite author: al fresco lunches on Spanish mountainsides, bull fighting, tales of the First World War and the Spanish Civil War, filled my head with images, people and places that I wanted to see and know.

Yet, how could I satisfy this craving for travel and adventure? My prospects were not looking good. Married in my senior year at Hunter College and needing a job desperately, the only occupation open to me was teaching. Fortunately I had taken nine credits of Education Courses, which entitled me to a substitute license to teach Junior High School English in the New York City School system. I was finding it very hard to land a teaching job. I was five foot four inches tall and weighed one hundred and twenty pounds soaking wet. I looked like a junior high school kid! Attempting to add a little maturity to my appearance I grew a moustache, and with a little fill-in from my wife's eyebrow pencil it didn't look half bad.

Every school I applied to just was not interested in my joining their faculty. One Principal, a lady, and a very tough, street-wise New Yorker, said, "You know, Mr. Salimbene, many of our students are bigger than you. How would you handle that?" Well, I huffed and puffed and said something to the effect, that I was sure I could gain the respect of the students by showing them I could help them improve their lives and achieve their dreams, yada, yada… "Well", she responded as she showed me to the door, "Sometimes short people have a Napoleonic complex and do quite well." And that was the last I heard from her. In fairness to her the school was located in Spanish Harlem and the police presence was quite evident. On my way to her office, a rather imposing black officer said in an aggressive tone, "Hey, where you think you're going?" I turned around with as much dignity as possible and said, "I am going to a job interview with the Principal." His reply, "Oh, shit, man, I thought you were one of the kids!"

In spite of rejection after rejection, once again I desperately checked the 'jobs available list' at the Board of Education on Chambers Street, and to my surprise, saw there was an opening for a Junior High School English teacher! The school was located a couple of blocks from our house on Avenue A and 12th St. I went to the school and was immediately ushered into the Principal's office. Mr. Sallen had a stack of papers piled on his desk, and he silently waved me to a chair across from his desk. After a while he looked up from his task and brusquely asked me what I wanted. I explained I was there to apply for the English position.

He looked at me appraisingly and asked, " Are you married?" Several seconds passed. The question threw me and I mumbled, "Yes, Sir." His next question threw me into further turmoil. "And what did you do that for?" I stuttered, "I love the girl!" His reply was simply, "OK, You got the job, Mister Salimbene. Come in on Monday. We'll show you a training film and introduce you to your class." I leapt out of the chair and offered my hand and as he rose to shake mine, we looked at each other eyeball to eyeball! We were the same exact height. I didn't know it at the time but we both were at a crossroads. His long career was ending and mine was just beginning.

The following Monday I went into the school office. It was a big open plan space with about five secretaries and parents clustered around their desks. I announced myself to the receptionist. She called over the Assistant Principal who was built like Arnold Schwarzeneger wearing bottle bottom glasses. I explained to him that the Principal had hired me on Friday. The AP looked down at me, complete shock written on his pock marked face. He appeared genuinely stunned when he turned to the room at large and in a booming voice cried out, "Will you look at who he hired? Will you look at what Sallen did to me? Drawing my five foot four to full height and with as much dignity as I could muster I said, "He hired me and said that I m supposed to see a training film."

For a minute I felt sorry for him because I thought that he was going to break down and cry. "There is no training film." he croaked. "Follow me!" he barked. Literally dragging me down a corridor we quick stepped to what sounded like a riot emanating from one of the classrooms. "Dear God, don't let this be my class." I prayed over and over again as we moved towards the murderous cacophony. He threw open the door and the students froze in place, reminiscent of a game we used to call 'Statues'. They were fixed in attitudes of mayhem and violence. Hands around each others throats, fists cocked, legs connected with all parts of the anatomy and those were just the girls! He unceremoniously shoved me into the room and announced, "This is your new teacher!" As he exited, he slammed the door. I learned later that I was the third teacher that this particular class had gone through. This was my introduction to the New York City Public School system.

Educated in Catholic Schools I had much to learn, but in a year and a half 'Arnold' declared me a "strong" teacher, which meant I took care of any classroom problems and didn't bother him. In the year and a half I worked there, I became interested in the teaching of English as a Second Language. The majority of my students were Hispanic and many of them were illiterate, although they had been in and out of the school system for years. The English books we were given were totally unsuitable and I knew that there had to be a methodology to help them learn English. I started taking courses in the teaching of English as a Foreign or Second Language at The New School for Social Research and later Teachers College, Columbia University.

My dream to travel was dormant but still very much alive. I had gotten an application for the Peace Corps but I was turned off because, if I recall correctly, it was at least 30 pages long. It seemed they wanted to know everything about me just short of whether I wore boxers or briefs. One evening in my last class to complete my M.A. a fellow student had an application, which she said was for a Fulbright Grant. I expressed interest and she gave it to me because she wasn't going to apply. The Fulbright Program was established in 1946 by the late Senator J. William Fulbright of Arkansas. It was, and is still today an extremely prestigious educational exchange program sponsored by the U. S. government. It is designed to increase mutual understanding between the people of the United States and the people of other countries. When I got home I filled the application out, got my references in order and sent it off. It was one page, front and back. My kind of application. I had applied for a grant to teach English in Spain. The previous year Suzanne and I had spent a summer in Barcelona, training Spanish teachers of English. We loved Spain and made many good friends and were quite anxious to return.

Within a very short time a reply came back that all the grants for Spain had been filled but would I be interested to be an alternate for Greece. By that time thanks to Suzanne I was teaching English as a Second Language at the New School for Social Research and had a number of wonderful Greek students who were planning to apply for entrance to U.S. universities. I quickly agreed to be an alternate. Within a week I had a request to go to the English Speaking Union for an interview. The woman who interviewed us was charming and over tea told us more about the program and what we could expect living in a new culture. At the conclusion of the interview she announced that she was satisfied we would be a credit to the Fulbright Program and she was going to give us the highest recommendation. Our adventure had begun.

Suzanne and I

From the moment we boarded the ship, 'Queen Frederica', our education about our host country began. We had learned some basic vocabulary and practiced the few words that we had learned from <u>Divry's Greek English Dictionary</u>, which was one of the best English-Greek dictionaries at the time. The waiters and the crew treated us like family. If you didn't like something they would quickly bring a substitute. Like my mother, they became very concerned when your plate was not completely devoid of all food. Whenever we used our limited and fractured Greek vocabulary they would respond by complimenting us and marveling over the fact that we had only been studying the language for such a short time and we were already 'fluent'. The cuisine was Greek and served in massive quantities. There was nothing to dislike: succulent lamb, avgo lemono (egg lemon) soup, mousaka, pasticcio, anginares (artichokes), bean soup, mousharis kokinisto (veal in red sauce), domates and piperies yemistes (stuffed tomatoes and peppers) and on and on.

Jimmy and Vicky and Johnny and his wife

We met two families: Jimmy and Vicki and Johnny and Helen who were returning to Greece after having lived in the United States for about ten years. Jimmy had worked in the restaurant business and then he and his wife had opened a hair salon in Pennsylvania. The family spoke excellent English. Jimmy's English was fluent and Vicki had a charming accent. They were delightful people and we enjoyed their company. They became part of our "parea" or company and we spent time with them during the day and dined with them at night. They seemed to balance family and social life effortlessly. They had fared well in the US. but they missed their families and wanted to return, especially in time for Jimmy's brother's wedding which we were invited to attend. This was a recurrent theme with all of our Greek American friends. They had to deal with the strong pull of family ties and their longing for Greece.

In my Italian family there was no nostalgia for Italy. It was only a place that had bad memories. The "old country" held nothing but hunger and suffering. I had been raised as an "American". My parents spoke Italian to each other but my sister and I were never encouraged to learn. Obviously my parents had suffered discrimination and they wanted us to become part of the melting pot. My mother once told me that if anyone would ask what I was, I was to tell them that I was an American. Growing up in the Bronx in an Irish-Catholic, Jewish neighborhood I was unaware of any prejudice. I cannot remember ever hearing an ethnic slur from friends or playmates even as a joke. We were all Americans, part of the melting pot. It was years later in the 60's that people became aware of their roots and wanted to be hyphenated Americans: Greek-American, Irish-American, Italian-American. The melting pot image was replaced with the crazy quilt. Later on in meeting Greeks I found a different case entirely. The older immigrant from Greece always lived with the idea that he would be able to return to the mother country and live in a style that he had become used to in the United States. Greek children were encouraged to speak Greek at home and English on the outside.

The other couple in our "parea" was Johnny and Helen. They had two beautiful daughters around the ages of 12 and 14. Johnny had owned a string of dry cleaning establishments and had bought into the American Dream. He was a compulsive worker and heavy smoker who ended up losing half of his stomach through overwork and stress. Their plan was to not only return to Greece but to return to his village in northern Epirus where the wife, a Greek American woman born in the States, nervously said that their new house had the only indoor toilet in the village! The girls were going to attend the village school and Johnny was going to live the life of the successful returned native son, hunting and spending his idle moments in the coffee house, "kafenion".

I still remember the day that I happened to be in John's stateroom and he casually showed me an attaché case filled with dollars. He fixed me with a hard stare and told me that he wanted to help me get settled in Greece and there was one piece of advice that I had to understand and never forget: I was never, under any circumstances, to ....trust a Greek. This was delivered with all seriousness punctuated by his thick, black eyebrows and moustache seeming to come together to emphasize what he was saying. He went on to say that I could always trust him, but no other Greek. All Greeks were deceitful, lying bastards according to my new friend. I found this information a little disconcerting but accepted it and filed it away for future reference. Thankfully it was never borne out to be true.

I later learned that Johnny and his family left Greece after a year. They could not adjust to the "primitive" nature of life in his village. However, Jimmy and Vicki stayed on in Greece and they did very well in the food service business. Several years later they had another boy. All three children went to the States for their undergraduate education, returned to Greece and followed successful and rewarding careers.

The 'Queen Frederika' docked in Piraeus on August 25, 1965. It was pandemonium. Passengers were attempting to disembark and well wishers were trying to get on board to welcome them. Porters were hurtling through the crowd like pin balls carrying off baggage. There were tears of joy and laughter as families came together. The first thing I noticed was the color of the sky. There was no pollution. It was a deep blue unlike the skies of New York. Everything around us seemed more vivid and intense in this clear light. Vendors were selling souvlaki and roasting nuts. The air was filled with delicious smells along with the briny odors of the harbor and the smoke from the ship as the engines were shut down. We bade goodbye to our new friends and agreed to meet Jimmy and Vicky the following week at their brother's wedding. They were our first friends and we would remain so for thirty years.

Through all this turmoil we found a young Greek woman whom Suzanne had befriended in New York. She was scheduled to fly back to Greece before us and had promised to meet us upon our arrival. She was there with her fiancé. They whisked us through customs and we drove into the city. The traffic seemed chaotic, everyone driving with mad abandon. The horn seemed to have replaced the brake pedal. Unbeknownst to us the Director of the Fulbright Program had driven out to meet us but we were long gone by the time he had arrived. Clearly he was not amused but he was quite gracious and welcoming when he came to see us at the hotel.

During this time Greece was beginning its full recovery from the Second World War and the terrible Civil War that had followed. Hostilities had not ended until 1949. Americans in general were respected and admired. "You are an American from New York, perhaps you know my cousin Petros who lives in Queens?" It seemed everyone had a relative who lived in New York or Chicago and was doing quite well. When we arrived in Athens there were riots and the whiff of tear gas in the air. Elections were being held and there were two rival parties headed by Constantine Karamanlis and George Papandreou. Greece has always been politically volatile, but I don't intend to speak of politics but of the people and our life in this period. As a side note, however, on a visit thirty four years later the elections were on and the two parties were still led by a Karamanlis and a Papandreou. Karamanlis' mantle had been handed down to a nephew and in the case of Papandreou a son now represented the family 'business'.

Fulbright ID

There must have been twenty-five or thirty Fulbrighters that year who would be teaching or doing research in the two main cities of Athens and Thessaloniki. We received an orientation and were generally wined and dined. On our second evening in

Athens we were invited to the home of the U.S. Ambassador. The drinks flowed as the waiters were very generous with the duty free booze to which the Embassy had access. One of the professors from a well known U.S. university was imbibing rather recklessly and I noticed that he was unsteady on his feet as he tried to focus on a pretty redhead. We were called to dinner. It was a buffet and as we lined up the professor happened to be in front of me. As he approached one of the chafing dishes he slurred, "Whas that?" and dipped his hand into the grilled chicken for a taste. I had a feeling that a combination of jet lag and booze would be the undoing of the eminent professor. We sat at bridge tables and he was, unfortunately, seated next to one of the embassy wives who was a heavy drinker. The waiters knew that her glass needed constant attention but the only guest at the table who was keeping up with her was the already inebriated professor. Now the embassy wife could hold her liquor and she had a little parlor trick that she performed when in her cups. When introduced to her she would look at you and say, "How nice to meet you, Mr. Salimbene, George," pause for effect, "And your charming wife," pause for effect, "Suzanne!" It was a pretty impressive feat drunk or sober. She clearly did her homework beforehand.

At the conclusion of dinner the Ambassador rose and welcomed us. He noted that the room was decorated with the works of famous American artists and he was certain that we would represent America as well as the work of the artists who graced the walls of the residence. There was polite applause and he invited us into the salon for coffee and liqueurs. We all rose but for the hapless professor who was head down in his mousaka. He was ignominiously carried out by two hefty colleagues. Feet dragging on the carpet, he attempted a pie eyed smile and wave at the guests as he was taken back to his hotel.

This same professor later returned from a Christmas holiday to Turkey and called on the Director of the Program to wish him seasons greetings. By way of greeting he said to the director that he would like to introduce his wife. The director smiled and was about to say that, of course, he had met his wife, but the lady in question was not the wife he had met at the beginning of the year! No one except one of the Greek drivers, Yiannis, had the nerve to ask what happened to wife number one. When queried by Yiannis, the professor said that they had been married thirty-five years and that was long enough. That silenced the ever curious Yiannis.

Years later my next memorable embassy experience involved Melina Mercouri, a famous Greek actress, who was appointed Minister of Culture years later after the Junta passed into history. We had been invited to the embassy for some celebration and suddenly Melina made her entrance. Everything and everyone seemed to gravitate towards her. There was a radiance, a magnetism about the woman. Her presence seemed to fill the room, and suddenly she looked at me and her face lit up, a pathway cleared. She was heading directly towards me. Not in my wildest moment could I imagine that Melina Mercouri of *'Never on Sunday'* fame would have any interest in me or even recognize me for that fact! Perhaps she had seen or heard about my school? Perhaps one of my enthusiastic students had spoken to her about a "wonderful and caring" headmaster? Just as she arrived in front of me she unceremoniously and vigorously elbowed me out of the way and flew into the arms of a tall gentleman standing behind me who had clearly been the object of her attention all the while. Fortunately I didn't make a fool of myself by reaching out to embrace her! God knows what chaos would have ensued.

Every day in Athens was a new experience for us. I was very excited by the thought of teaching at the University, but when opening day approached we were told not to bother to show up for classes because the students were on strike. It was not an unusual situation we were assured. They struck quite regularly for political reasons, but the latest strike was focused on the number of times that a student could re-take the final exam if he or she failed. The students wanted to be able to take the finals as many times as was needed to pass. This was unheard of to us, but it got even wilder. Students did not have to attend class! They only had to show up for the final and pass it. A colleague warned me that I might have 20 students attending on a daily basis but in fact the number was more like 50 or 60 who would show up for the exam. As a result we had to prepare copies of final exams far in excess of the number of students attending the different courses. The fact that my students were on strike and I was not working caused a little stress in the Salimbene family. Suzanne had found a teaching job at a private college. So, she went off to work every day and I was left to plan my expeditions to the museums and various archaeological sites throughout the city. Classes finally started just before Christmas.

The English Department was the only department in the University that required students to attend classes. But we could not prevent those who didn't attend from taking the final. They would fill up the testing room and slowly one by one they would hand in the test booklet and answer sheet once they saw that simply reading the assigned books was not enough to pass the test. We were also advised to watch out for cheating, not plagiarism necessarily but good old-fashioned look over the shoulder of your neighbor to see what he has written down. This stemmed from the teaching style employed in the high schools. There could be as many as fifty or sixty students to a high school class and a student was on his own. The teacher would give a few examples and then the students were required to do the reading and memorization. Students were given an oral grade as well as a written exam and perhaps once a week or once every two weeks required to stand up and regurgitate verbatim what they had memorized from the book. In a system like this a student needed all of the help that she or he could get from their friends. One advantage that they had was phenomenally well trained memories. They were always after us to teach them what was going to be on the test. Everything was rated by the question, "Will this be on the test?" Generally the students were extremely bright and hard working and they learned in spite of the pedagogy. Another aspect of the cheating was the fact that you helped a friend no matter what. That's what friends were for. If you didn't extend help, you weren't a friend. Being aware of this cultural nuance we tried to make the testing situation as fair as possible and to limit the opportunities for cheating.

My University students

One of the hardest mini-courses that we had to teach was on a Wednesday afternoon. It was called "English Conversation". The students were very reluctant to be forthcoming and they would never disagree with you. It was like pulling teeth. I asked one of my students with whom I had become friendly, to give me some ideas that would stimulate sparkling dialogue. He suggested themes on love and marriage since there were a majority of women in our classes.

Following his suggestion I went off to class and introduced the question of what they thought the most desirable age was for marriage. The class came alive. Many believed that you should marry someone older because young men could not afford a wife. Others believed that someone of the same age made for the best understanding between a man and a woman. The hour flew by. When we had finished I thanked them for their participation but one young girl looked very forlorn. "Why so unhappy, Sophia, wasn't it an exciting class?" Her reply floored me, but she was serious, "No sir because you didn't tell us what to do." After a moment's hesitation I said, "Look if anyone is contemplating marriage in the next couple of months come and see me, but if that isn't the case just think over the things that we have been talking about!"

The days flew by and before we knew it, it was Christmas. But far from the Yuletide spirit that we were used to in the States, we learned that in Greece at that time it was a non-event. There was no White Christmas and holiday entertainment. We couldn't even find decorations until, by accident, we found a few forlorn Christmas ornaments in one of the main squares, Omonia Square, the day before Christmas. The fir tree was not a recognized symbol for Christmas. For the Greeks it was a miniature fishing boat decorated with lights. The main holiday in our new country was Easter and that matched the preparation and ceremony accorded to western Christmas and more so. There were candlelight processions, whole lambs were roasted over open fires, tubs of hard boiled eggs were dyed red, and fireworks and shotguns were fired off into the air.

Our everyday lives were very exciting and pleasant. We bought white and red "Demestica "Achaia Claus wine in a straw wrapped bottle that was called a "dramizan" about a gallon and a half. It was a fine, hearty wine that left no after effects (stuns but won't kill) and went well with our new diet. It cost 70 or 90 drachmas (three dollars) and did not put a dent in our food budget. In those days there were thirty drachmas to one dollar. The only beer that you could drink was "FIX" and there were none of the American brands of Coke or Seven Up. The only exception that I remember was Fanta; an orange drink that tasted like real oranges. The only other soft drinks were limited to a "lemonada" (lemonade) or a "portokalada"(orangeade) which were bottled by the FIX company.

The Athens Central Market

The fresh vegetables were delicious but you could never find anything out of season. When cabbage was in that was all you could find until the next crop was ready. But what a fresh taste and odor the vegetables had! Their freshness was overwhelming when we compared it to what we had been used to getting in the States from the local A&P. It took us a while to get used to buying "kilos"(2.2lbs.). Initially we used the kilo in the same manner that we used the lb. But we soon learned the difference: a kilo of spinach was a formidable amount of spinach that was way beyond the capacity of two people to consume. There were two kinds of yogurt: cows milk and goats milk. Both kinds had a thick crust on top and were strong for my palate until I started lacing them with fresh honey. The yogurt made from cows milk was less strong in taste. Every time we bought cheese it was an adventure and a taste treat. I could never remember any of the names except for the well known "feta" and "kasseri". Milk came in little pint bottles with a silver seal on top. The cream would separate and remain at the top and you had to shake it up, but I found the taste too pungent and I did not care for it. Butter was not what we were used to in the states and it had a strong cheesy taste rather like the milk. Buying a cut of meat that was recognizable was a real challenge. None of the cuts that the butchers displayed resembled anything that we were used to from home. If you bought meat that was off the bone they would throw in the bone because the claim was that they bought the animal and the bones. It was all legal.

There were no big super markets in Athens at the time. You shopped in the bakery for your bread. The bakery also cooked your dinner or lunch for a small fee. Many homes at the time did not have ovens, so for a few drachma you brought your prepared food to the bakery and they cooked it in their oven for you. There was the local sweet shop (zacharoplasteon) for all sorts of confectionary sweets and coffee. There were neighborhood stores for fish, wine, household goods, and the ubiquitous grocery store (bakaliko) where you could buy cheese, delicatessen meats, yoghurt and canned goods. The neighborhood kiosk (periptero) sold everything else from matches to prophylactics. Matches were a state monopoly and came in little wooden boxes and were manufactured in one of the Scandinavian countries if I remember correctly. In each store you were greeted by name and you responded by enquiring after the owner's health and family. Your neighborhood was your community. No one was anonymous.

When you went to the cinema there was an intermission in the middle of the film. I found that practice very curious since in the U.S. there was only an intermission in the legitimate theater. I later learned that one of the reasons for the intermission was that it provided time for the projectionist to set up the second reel which was sometimes brought from another cinema across town. They timed it so that one cinema started just as the neighboring one was concluding. In the summer time there were outdoor cinemas because there was no air-conditioning. You sat out under the stars and usually watched re-runs that you might have missed during the winter. You could buy beers and cheese pies which you brought back to your seat. In crowded neighborhoods with apartment building surrounding the cinema, the local people sat out on their balconies and watched from the comfort of their own homes. All the western films were in English with Greek subtitles. Sometimes the sound was low because people didn't need it, but you could ask the projectionist to raise the sound and he was usually perfectly amenable. But because of the translation sometimes people laughed in the wrong place and then you lost the spoken dialogue.

One of the couples had brought their pet poodle with them. This created quite a sensation when they took it for a walk. There were very few dogs in Athens at the time. The general consensus was that they were disease bearing and dangerous. This attitude was fostered by the war years and the scarcity of food. The idea of feeding pets when the general population was faced with starvation just did not make any sense to the average Greek. A crowd always gathered when they took the dog for a walk. I am sure the fact it was a miniature poodle and the wife was a dazzling red head, also increased the curiosity.

Suzanne went out one day wearing slacks and came back ten minutes later in a panic. She said that men were approaching her and cars had actually stopped and men got out and spoke to her. We couldn't figure out whether all the attention had to do with the fact that she was obviously a foreigner or perhaps the slacks had something to do with it. We later learned that virtuous women did not wear slacks. When Suzanne got her driver's license again she received a lot of attention because there were not that many women drivers at the time. It seemed every day there was something new to learn and we often found ourselves the center of attention.

We decided that we had to buy a car to better get around visiting the various archaeological sites. I didn't have a driver's license and as a result I had to apply for a Greek one. I learned that before you could take the test you had to have driving lessons from a private school. My teacher was a merchant seaman who was land based until his next ship sailed. While on land he made extra money by teaching people how to drive. His methods were a little unusual. He played loud bouzouki music and insisted on trying to stick cigarettes in my mouth while I was navigating traffic. He explained that it would relax me. I had to explain every time that I didn't smoke and jamming cigarettes in my mouth distracted me and made me very nervous. While driving around he would command me to stop and he would jump out and engage or try to engage a young woman in conversation. He would invariably get rebuffed and get back into the car and announce, "My sister!". On the day before I was scheduled to take the test at his direction we drove out of Athens to a large vacant field. He got out of the car and came around to the driver's side and said, "Now, Yourgo(George), I want you to drive around the field in a circle....in reverse!" This was said with great gravity and concern as if he was a flight instructor telling me to take the 747 up for a solo flight.

In reverse? I had been asking him to let me park, but he kept saying that it wasn't necessary. I couldn't conceive of a driving exam without parking. Finally he reluctantly agreed while we were on a hill. I managed to park and felt that I could manage the task if called upon. As instructed I backed up and drove around the field in reverse. When I got back to him he exclaimed to some other instructors and students who had arrived as I was circumnavigating the field, "Look at this man! In only twelve lessons he drove around in a complete circle!" The bystanders seemed impressed. I was just puzzled. The next morning I arrived at the motor vehicle office and three inspectors got in the back seat. My trusty teacher was sitting next to me looking very tense. I was instructed to drive out onto the highway, turn around and head back to the motor vehicle building and drive to the back of the building. To my surprise I saw an enormous field with about thirty cars all driving around in reverse. Some of the cars were going off in tangents and spiraling almost out of control. In this dust storm were referees supervising the cars that failed to complete the magic circle. I passed with flying colors.

However, my trial wasn't over yet. I had to take a written exam for which I had studied. Foreigners were allowed to take the exam for illiterates which consisted of comic book type pictures of different driving situations. When I went to take the written exam the clerk asked if there was anyone who spoke English. A young woman came forward. I was puzzled because it was multiple choice without any writing. However, the choices were in the Greek alphabet, so the clerk must have thought I couldn't mange even that. At any rate I made my first selection and my second selection and on the third question the young girl asked me if I was sure of my answer. I replied that I was pretty sure. She informed me that she had taken the test earlier and knew for a fact that I had chosen the wrong answer. With her help I got a perfect score and weeks letter a Greek drivers license. With the license came an eight by ten piece of paper with a capital 'N' which you were supposed to put in the back window of your car. This announced to the driving public that you were a 'new' driver. Far from providing any protection, I never used it because it seemed to me that other drivers tended to cut you off or lean on their horns when they saw the 'N'.

For the first couple of weeks we lived on souvlaki or 'giro' because it was cheap and easy to pronounce. It was cooked on a vertical spit and consisted of huge chunks of skewered lamb that was then shaved in thin strips. The shavings were placed in "pita" bread with onions and tomatoes. After a while the onions started to get to me and I asked my Greek teacher to teach me how to say "without onions". I learned that it was "horis kremidia"! Now in the early days of trying to learn Greek we passed through a stage of not wanting to speak unless it was word perfect. Then we had to deal with the unreasonable feeling that people were laughing at us. They certainly stared at us because they knew we were foreigners by dress and language. The Greeks were very uninhibited when it came to checking each other out. Every new situation that we found ourselves in was fraught with anxiety and it seemed required us to exert all of our courage. I learned the phrase, "Horis kremidia" word perfect and the next day I lined up for my souvlaki chanting the mantra..."horis kremidia"! It was my turn and I said "Ena souvlaki, parakalo, horis kremidia." (One souvlaki, please, without onions.) And because of the street noise the fellow behind the counter fired back "With onions?". And that request for a confirmation threw me for a loop. I hadn't rehearsed that and I took the easiest way out and said "Nai" (Yes!) and with a sinking heart I saw the onions go into my souvlaki.

Athenians willingly spoke English and if you were in a shop having a hard time communicating with the owner he would send out for someone who spoke English. I was determined to use the few words that I had learned and was frustrated when the person I was speaking to would answer in English or send out for help and a ten year old boy would come in to act as my translator. One day I went into a shop and asked the owner, in what I thought was good Greek, if he sold needles. All it required from him was a yes, "nai", or no, "oxi". But he fixed me with a neutral look and raised his chin slightly. I thought he didn't understand me. So, I changed the phrasing "Needles you have?" This time he raised his head and clicked his tongue. Confusion on my part. What the heck is going on? I tried again: "You, needles have"? This time the head went back, the eyes closed and the tongue clicked. But I wouldn't retreat. Normally I would have said, "Yes, thank you." and beat a strategic retreat. But this time I was determined to stick it out till I got to the bottom of this linguistic mystery. I reverted to the age old tactic: get louder and simplify the request. "Needles" I shouted making a sewing motion. This time with a show of impatience which was certainly justified. He looked me in the eye for a second shot his head back. raised his eyebrows, clicked his tongue and said "Oxi!". Eureka! I went outside and told Suzanne that I had learned the sign for "No" in Greek which none of my teachers had ever bothered to teach me. But my confidence was slowly being strengthened. Another time I went into my favorite neighborhood taverna and saw that on display in the refrigerator were what appeared to me to be scallops. I asked the owner what they were and he mumbled 'omilettita'. Now I heard 'omelet'. So, I asked him how he made the "omelet". There were other customers around and I could see that he was uncomfortable and wanted me to place my order and move on. But I was not about to be budged. I asked him what kind of eggs they were. I had never seen anything like them. They are not eggs he replied and enunciated, "They are 'omilettita'." Then he made a universal gesture, hand cupped at the waist and raised and lowered as if there was something heavy in his hand. I then realized that I was looking at 'rocky mountain oysters'. I later learned that the word I had mistaken for 'omelet' was 'omilettita' or the 'unmentionables', lamb testicles.

Our first apartment on Niaidon Street

Our first apartment was a "retiree" (top floor) on Niaidon Street opposite Lykavitos hill and across from the Hilton Hotel. The young woman who had met us at the ship helped us find it. Hunting for apartments was difficult if you didn't read and speak Greek. Signs were pasted to lampposts in different neighborhoods: 'Enoikiazete' (Renting) or 'Politai' (Selling). Written on the paper sign was the address or telephone number of the person renting or selling. You called them up and made an appointment to go and see the place. We were determined to get a view. Finally we found an apartment with a truly magnificent view of Lykavitos, the Acropolis and Piraeus in the distance. Everything was dug up in front of the house and the theodoros (conceirge) Bobbis told us that one day it would be a park and sure enough about fifteen years later it became Byron Park with a bust of the English poet Lord Byron in it. It was a very small park on Vas. Konstantinou. It was a noisy area but the view made up for the noise. From our back window we had a view of the mountain Hymettos which turned purple in the twilight. During the winter it was cold because the Athenians only heated the apartments several hours in the morning, midday and then again at night usually until 10 p.m. It was not unusual to visit people in the winter and be greeted by your host who was wearing an overcoat. We used electric heaters to supplement the heat because it got quite cold in the winter and could even snow.

It was great fun to explore and try to buy produce and cook our meals. We had brought an electric frying pan from the US which was 220 current and we cooked all of our meals in it. We made some excellent meals with that pan that you could fry and bake in. I recall that we had a two burner electric hot plate to supplement our pan. We often ate out because food was cheap and we were well paid. I think that year I was paid the equivalent of about $500.00 a month which went a very long way.

When we arrived in Athens, one of the first things that we did was open a checking account and a savings account at Citibank in Syntagma Square. We thought that we would be paying for everything by check. At that time credit cards had not come into use. The first time the landlord came to collect the rent, I gave him a check and he looked at it as if it was some form of alien life form. "What is this?" He asked a Greek friend who was visiting us. The friend explained the purpose of the check and he reluctantly accepted it and asked our friend to ask us to have cash the next time because checks appeared to be too much trouble. We ended up throwing the checks away because no one used them and everyone was reluctant to accept them for payment. It was strictly a cash and carry society. Several years later when we purchased land on Evia I went to the bank and thought that I would get a cashier's check but I was informed that I had to take cash. It was the equivalent of five thousand dollars and at the time the largest note was one thousand drachmas or roughly thirty three dollars. Suddenly I realized why most of the men carried shoulder bags or for want of a better term 'handbags'. The teller took pity on me and gave me three legal sized envelopes that I was able to cram most of the money into and then I tried to stuff them into my pants pocket. Pant styles at the time were tight fitting and I ended up walking out of the bank thoroughly misshapened. I hobbled back to the car and made a mental note to pick up a 'manbag'.

Tavernas were the places to eat. They were extremely inexpensive and the food was delicious. When you walked into a taverna you usually walked through the kitchen and checked out the dishes to see what you wanted to eat that night. The food was all cooked on the premises and it was simple but good. In the summer most of the tavernas had outside courtyards and you would go out and sit under the stars. Some yards were surrounded by apartment buildings but the neighbors would usually ignore the diners. From time to time a strolling guitarist would come through and if the hour was late people would start to sing folksongs that everyone knew. To accompany the food there was retsina the famous Greek wine which was very palatable and complemented the rich food . Some foreigners did not like retsina because it had a slight taste of resin. This came from the fact that Greek wine had been traditionally stored in pine barrels that were not aged so that the wine picked up the taste of the resin. Over the centuries people grew to like it and as a result the tradition grew. There were other wines without resin (aretsinoto) for people who did not care for retsina.

A typical meal went something like this: First the wine was ordered and then you would order the 'mezedhes' or appetizers. Some of the appetizers were peculiar to a particular taverna and others were standard. So you could order from a wide selection. For example, giant beans in tomato sauce, fava (mashed chick peas), peasants' salad, fried eggplant, fried zucchini, snails, fried mushrooms, spetsofai (sausage and peppers), 'kokkoretsi' (lung, liver, kidney, heart of the lamb wrapped in the lambs' intestines) and barbecued on a spit, grilled meatballs, sausage, marides (tiny fish fresh fried), octopus, feta cheese, haloumi (a Cypriot cheese that was fried), croquettes, and fresh salads of romaine lettuce and cabbage. After this was devoured then you were ready to order your entrée from the grill or many of the good things that I had been introduced to on the boat. We ate far too much but we were young and didn't seem to gain much weight at least in the early years. These meals would cost between two and three dollars.

THESSALONIKI

AFTER AN EVENTFUL YEAR IN ATHENS at the University we decided that we wanted to stay for a second year. We enjoyed our work and the people, we earned a good income, and we could afford to travel in Greece and outside. Dining out was so cheap, it was actually cheaper to eat out then to prepare a meal for two people! We were in a foreign country and literally something new was going on every day. Travelling in Greece was exciting because the different places were so beautiful and untouched by tourism that we felt we were discovering some of the archaeological sites for the first time. For me it was the thrill of being on a frontier. The only complication of staying a second year was that the Director of the Fulbright Foundation said that we would have to go to the University of Thessaloniki about 500 kilometers north of Athens. Suzanne threw a fit. She said that the city was a hole and that we would not be happy there. She was quite miserable about the move because she had a job in Athens and was settled in. She had even started dancing with a well known Greek folk dance group which was a singular honor. I was more relaxed since it was a way of staying in Greece and I didn't believe that Thessaloniki could be that backward.

We had purchased a VW Beetle. The plan was to have our few possessions shipped up to Thessaloniki on the day that we were planning to drive up so that the next day we could have our furniture delivered to our new apartment. The plan was simple but the intervention of the gods must always be reckoned with. It was a very hot day in June when we started out and the car was loaded. We got as far as Thebes, about an hour and a half from Athens when there was an ominous rumbling from the engine and then the two little lights on the dash went on indicating that we were out of oil and the engine was hot. In those days our Greek wasn't great and there was no road assistance of any kind. Finally a man came along in a pick up truck and explained that he was a mechanic. He towed us back to his shop which was located in an abandoned, crumbling school house. The only thing that he could communicate to us was that the situation was very serious, "poli sovaro". There were no translators about and I could not get any more information, so I risked it and told him to go ahead and find out what was wrong. He started by taking the engine apart piece by piece.

It was like watching a loved one being disemboweled before your eyes. First the fuel and oil were drained and then bit by bit the engine was taken apart and the pieces hurled into a cardboard box, until the crankshaft was revealed. We had blown the crankshaft and that was the heart of the engine. He quoted me a phenomenal amount of money to fix the car, more than I had paid for it. Frantic, I got on the phone and called the dealer who had sold it to me. He told me to calm down and get the car towed back to Athens and they would repair it in their own workshop, which at least did not look like it had been on the target list of the Luftwaffe. How do we get the car back to Athens I wailed there is no AAA? He told me to find a trucker and they would bring us back to Athens for about 3,000 drachmas($100). Meanwhile the Theban bandit who had picked me up wanted 1,000 drachmas for the "work" that he had done. I finally decided to pay the ransom and get the hell out of Thebes. I remembered my mythology and it was before Thebes that Oedipus got into a lot of trouble. We found a truck driver who agreed to load our car onto the back of his truck and we rode back to Athens in our Beetle sitting high and dry. It took us about four days to get the car repaired in Athens before we started off again on our journey to Thessaloniki. In those days the trip took eight to ten hours if I remember correctly. The national road was two lanes and it was heavily traveled. Today it is a superhighway and the scene of frequent accidents because people drive too fast and take unnecessary chances, which in a way is part of the 'Greek reality'.

Our arrival in Thessaloniki was not auspicious. We had to travel by the Esso refinery and major highway work that created a tremendous amount of dust and noise. Once past that, the city seemed charming. Eventually we found a lovely apartment again through the help of a new friend. This was a young woman that Suzanne had met at our local dry cleaners. Roula had spent a year abroad through the auspices of the American Field Service. She spoke English and helped us get organized. Time and again strangers treated us like guests. After five minutes of introduction they became our hosts, going out of their way to help us.

The pier outside our apartment in Thessaloniki

Our apartment was right on the waterfront near a fish market. We were on the second floor and from our bedroom, actually from the bed, we could look out and see the Gulf of Thermaikos. Across the gulf was Mount Olympos. The apartment was very large with

35

three or four bedrooms. The bathroom did not have an outside window and the whole room was heavily mildewed and black and needed to be scrubbed down with bleach. The landlord said that he had rented it to some Japanese gentlemen and they were in the habit of steaming. Great, thought I. It wouldn't have killed them if they had washed down the place from time to time. Another feature that I remember that was true of apartments everywhere: they were painted in rainbow colors. You had a blue room, a green room, a yellow room, a rose room, and the kitchen was usually white. Otherwise the apartment was very sunny and it was literally a stone's throw away from the water. In the evening we would hear the fishing boats leave and then come back in the morning. They had a very distinctive sound. Not at all intrusive, just a dull thunk, thunk, thunk.

The first night in our new home we slept on the floor because we had no bedding or furniture. We used our camping gear and hoped that the moving van firm would bring our possessions the next day. In the morning the theodoros (concierge) called us and said that our possessions had arrived. We heard them huffing and puffing as they came up the stairs. One of the men was barefoot and manhandling an enormous sack of fertilizer. "What is this?" I queried.

"They are your things." The barefoot bearer replied.

"They are not my things. Furniture, my things are furniture." I struggled to explain.

When you are not proficient in a foreign language you are limited in your ability to swear and you must just keep repeating yourself, over and over again. In the end we had to go down to the warehouse and identify our things because no one could read the invoice that had been written in Athens. Who knows what the real reason was, but clearly our delay caused by the breakdown had contributed to the fact that our possessions had become lost or misplaced. We finally found them after an hour in a corner of the warehouse. Unbelievably everything was loaded on a motorcycle that had a small flat bed truck body. They were called "Kamikazes". Five minutes driving with them left you in no doubt about their name. Like their Japanese namesakes they exhibited a reckless disregard for life and limb.

View from our balcony

Thessaloniki was in a building boom and we had arrived at the right time. It was a lovely seaport town once you got past the Esso refinery and the construction of the main north south highway. It had a natural harbor and in 1966 the city was small enough to be able to walk anywhere or just hop a bus and get into town. The sunsets were magnificent and always set behind Mt. Olympos. You could order an ouzo on the waterfront and there was always a "meze"(appetizer) served with it. Out in the city we would inevitably run into friends or colleagues at the university. It had a small town feel but it was very cosmopolitan.

Fulbright and the British Council provided teachers to the University and my boss was a man by the name of Douglas Blackett.

He was head of the British Council. I later learned that he was from a "red brick university" not one of the elite institutions and he and his wife were 'Geordies' meaning that they came from northern England. I had never met any British people and my knowledge of them was limited to the cinema and the old World War II propaganda movies that I used to watch on daytime television. Jim Warner, The Fulbright Director came up to Thessaloniki to introduce me to Douglas who seemed very pleasant with his moustache, florid complexion and British accent. Jim asked Douglas what my duties would be and Douglas straightened his back and fixed me with a steely glance and said something to the effect of: "I charge Mr. Salimbene with the responsibility of improving the skills of our students to the highest standard." There were about four or five charges and I was at first petrified by his manner, but then a warm glow came over me and I was back in those wonderful movies with David Niven and Jack Hawkins. This is what it is like receiving your orders just before you go "over the top" and bash 'old Jerry' I thought to myself. I learned that he was a very warm-hearted man and I grew to like him although the British teachers on staff tended to scoff because of his 'background'. I was totally perplexed by the class consciousness of my new British friends.

Douglas and his wife endeared themselves to me when we invited them to our home for dinner one evening. We had prepared everything with painstaking care, our first British guests! We considered them so cosmopolitan and superior, everything had to be just right to show them that we were not the crass Yankees that we actually were! When the bell rang we rushed to the door and warmly welcomed them. Just as we were ushering them into the dining room, Douglas looked over our heads and said: I say George, the cat seems to have started on the hors d'oeuvres! We turned around and to our horror the cat was on the table helping itself to the herring that we had found that day in the market. Fortunately, the Blacketts were animal lovers and said, "Not to worry." and we got on with our meal. They were lovely, decent people whom we liked very much. Three years later Douglas was killed in a car crash in France while driving his children back to England. The irony was, that during the Second World War he had fought in France and had been captured at Dunkirk. He survived the war only to be killed in peacetime in France years later.

We had a small circle of friends from the University and other Fulbrighters. Some Fulbrighters had been assigned to the American Farm School and others to an American sponsored school Anatolia College. Basically everybody kept pretty close to the people that they worked with. Our group consisted of the British teachers from the Council and the Greek teachers who were teaching English at the University. Once in a while we would meet up with the other Fulbrighters. Eve was a British teacher from the Council and we were often invited to sumptuous meals at her house. She was a gourmet cook and whatever she served always tasted like ambrosia. After a meal we would drink more wine, play cards or word games late into the night.

I remember one New Year's Day. Suzanne had gone to Russia on an excursion and I had stayed behind because I didn't want to go to a colder clime especially winter in Russia. I remembered what had happened to Napoleon and Hitler! Eve and her boyfriend and I and one or two more friends went up to the top of the city walls overlooking the city and the harbor. We opened bottles of champagne and just sat there soaking up the sunshine and the beauty of the day. As was our custom we ended up at Eve's and she cooked something spectacular, mussels in a white wine sauce, no one wanted to go home after such a magical day. We started the usual card game and then just sat around talking nonsense and enjoying each others company.

It was a magical time and something was always happening. One Saturday morning I drove to the university, and I noticed that there wasn't a lot of traffic on the road. When I got to the roundabout in front of the Trade Center Exhibition Hall I found a tank sitting in the middle of the round about. The tracks had been let down from the vehicle and I noticed that it was sporting a large 50 caliber machine gun that was manned by a soldier, more startling there was a belt of ammunition loaded into the gun. I did not give it any further thought. After all, if a Greek army tank was going to break down why not right in the middle of a round about? I got to the university and I noticed that the students were flowing out of the buildings. This was not uncommon because we often had strikes and the students thought nothing of taking off for as long as it required for their demands to be accepted. I approached one of my girls and asked her what was happening. She replied that she could not explain in English and that it had something to do with the military taking over the government. Did she mean a "coup d'état"? She replied " I don't know the English word sir. The army has told us to go home." It was the 21st of April, 1967 and the Colonels had come to power.

This came about after weeks of political unrest. Many Greeks said that was what was needed because the Greeks are impossible to govern. But the majority felt that it was unjust and usurped the power of the people. I tried to stay out of political discussions. I felt that I had been invited into the country and any opinion that I had, I intended to keep to myself. Under the Colonels on the surface life went on without the political bickering, strikes and student demonstrations. The Americans were blamed for supporting the Junta if not actually organizing it. Years later it was revealed that the fine hand of the CIA was involved.

America's image was tarnished, but my Greek friends would blame the American government but not individual Americans. As I noted earlier there has always been a strong tie between Greece and the US because of the large number of immigrants that had settled in the US. I saw this strong friendship and respect eroded during the Junta years. After the Junta was overthrown, whether it was a right wing or socialist government, Greece never left NATO.

The Socialist government of Andreas Papandreou was very anti-American but it appeared that the Americans generally got what they wanted, the bases and the missiles remained until years later when they became unnecessary.

As an interesting aside, Andreas Papandreou the leader of the Socialist Party left Greece and immigrated to the US before the Second World War and served in the US Navy. He was a naturalized American and married an American woman and they had three children. Within my first month in Athens the Fulbright Director arranged a meeting at his home for the Fulbrighters to meet Andreas Papandreou who, I believe at that time, was Minister of Education in his father's government. His father, George Papandreou was then Prime Minister. Andreas spoke to us for more than an hour and was extremely pleasant. He spoke English with a slight accent. He described himself as a Stevensonian Democrat. For American liberals that meant the very highest standards of integrity and progressive politics. We listened to him and were literally spell bound. That evening someone remarked that it was a great loss to American politics that Andreas Papandreou had left the United States. The next night we learned that he addressed a rally in Piraeus and denounced the Americans, advocated closure of the bases, and an end to all U.S. influence. Rather naively I was appalled that a man one night could say that he was a Stevensonian democrat and then act like a demagogue the next. Many Greeks believed in him despite the fact that he was to all intents an American not born but educated and trained in the US. He had tremendous support for someone who suddenly appeared on the Greek political scene having spent the war years in the U.S. But he had been called back by his father and it was not uncommon for these political dynasties to self perpetuate. They voted him in again and again despite a major financial scandal, and a messy divorce. When he passed away the mantel was passed on to his son George, named after his grandfather.

A TRIP TO ISTANBUL

SHORTLY AFTER THE COUP, WE DECIDED TO DRIVE TO TURKEY for a holiday. We had been there once before in 1965 and we were looking forward to getting back to the opulence of the Grand Bazaar and seeing a bit of the countryside. We had been warned not to go to Turkey because the border between Greece and Turkey had only just been reopened. But we were desperate to get away from all the intrigue and tension. A friend of ours asked to come along. Jane was a fellow Fulbrighter and English teacher, a very attractive red head who was well-travelled and easy to be with, in all a good travelling companion. Suzanne and I both liked her very much. She had flair and exuded confidence. She dressed well and always had an admiring entourage of young Greek men following her around.

As I recall it was about a six hour drive from Thessaloniki to Istanbul. We had a new VW Bug and we made the trip without any adventures except when a huge trailer truck passed us at high speed and a chunk of gravel flew up and starred the windshield which fortunately did not shatter. When we arrived in Istanbul we found a hotel and parked the car in a garage because I did not want to drive any more than I had to in the city. The Turks made the Greeks look tame when it came to driving. They seemed to hurl themselves upon each other and constantly just manage to avoid a collision. I was sure that if I drove my new car around town it would be bashed to pieces.

We toured the city for about three days and on the last day of our stay we took the car out of the garage. We planned to drive to the area around the Blue Mosque where the black-market money changers hung out. We were going to convert our dollars to lira at a rate of about twelve to one. The official rate was about four to one. I exchanged money for all of us, being careful to select a dealer who looked honest. I settled on a ten year old who seemed to be doing a good business. Once our business was transacted I hustled back to the girls and we took off feeling quite daring. We drove along the Bosporus and had lunch at a quay side restaurant dining while watching the boats ply the strait. It was a lovely afternoon. Our plan was to return to the hotel, pack up and get an early night's sleep, leave the city early next morning and begin to sightsee, travelling to Ephesus, Troy and other archaeological places of importance. But the gods had other plans for us.

As we were driving back to our hotel, on one of the main streets, a man ran out from in front of a bus and literally hit me! I tried to avoid him and ended up in the oncoming lane of traffic. The man had been knocked flying and laid out in the street. A crowd had gathered but there were no policemen in sight. I got out and looked at the injured pedestrian but there was nothing that I could do for him. About a block away I saw a soldier directing traffic and I decided to run up to him and ask for help. He spoke no English and seemed reluctant to help me but I put on a pantomime and he very grudgingly came to see what was going on. In the meantime a crowd had gathered and later Jane told me that it was getting nasty because they thought that the driver, me, had run off. By the time I returned with the soldier in tow the police had finally showed up. No one spoke English except a young university student who came out of the crowd. He told me that he was going to the U.S. on a Fulbright grant in the Fall to study and he would come to the police station with me to translate. His English was not very good, but I gratefully accepted his help.

We drove to the police station in my car and found that no one there spoke any English. The police were very surly and intimidating, in their leather jackets and menacing looks. Jane and Suzanne were made very uncomfortable by the appraising glances of the policemen and they retired to a corner of the room. There was no one to explain what was going to happen. The student seemed to be taking a lot of abuse from the police for helping us. I called Suzanne over and slipped her the money that I had exchanged on the black market. I thought I would be taken off to the cells at any minute and the money was safer with the girls. Suddenly they produced a statement for me to sign. The student said that it was alright to sign, that it was just a basic description of the accident. I explained to him that I could not take his word for that because we were having difficulty in communicating. How could he adequately translate a legal document for me? I explained to him that I needed to see a representative of the American Embassy before I would sign anything. All of this was being explained in the simplest terms and as inoffensively as I could manage because he was our only friend. I asked him to ask the policeman to let me call the Embassy. He approached them with my request. They talked amongst themselves and laughed and then the boss who was a cross between Akim Timaroff and Telly Savalas, big on eye-brows but short on hair, rasped a reply which started everyone laughing again. The student translated that I could use the phone if I knew the number of the Embassy. I saw the embarrassment on his face. My heart sank. They were just toying with me. I was stuck.

I went back and told Suzanne that it didn't look very good because there were no phone books and I probably couldn't read them if I tried because I didn't know Turkish. Our only friend the student was getting very nervous from the way the police were treating him. Both Jane and Suzanne up until that moment had been very cool and that had helped me to keep hold of my own rising fear. Jane looked at me and with a smile to rival Giaconda, she said, "The number of the American Embassy is 445-369. I was incredulous. How did she know the number? She explained that she had called the embassy in the morning because there was a celebration for the Emir's birthday or something to that effect and she remembered the number. I went up to the desk tingling with anticipation. We weren't out of trouble but possibly help was at hand. I told the student that I wanted to use the phone. The police laughed and pointed to the phone. With trembling hand I dialed the number and my heart leapt when I heard the magic words, "American Embassy". I was connected to a consular officer and explained the situation as lucidly as I could. They assured me that someone would be coming down very soon. The student was getting ready to leave and I asked him for one more favor could he find out how the injured man was doing. Again a long conversation ensued punctuated by laughter and excited gesticulations. It ended on a universal note of laughter by the policemen present. The student looked at me mournfully and said, "They say that he is dead." The police were watching my face and again laughed when they saw the shock register. Part of the shock was from the thought, "How could they laugh about something like that? What kind of people are they?"

The accident occurred at about 3 p.m. By 4:30 a buttoned down Embassy representative arrived. After brief introductions he said, "Well, you are in serious trouble Mr. Salimbene." Statement of the bloody obvious I thought to myself. I don't need you to tell me that I am in deep trouble. But I held my tongue. This was no time to lose my cool; at the end of the day he was my only lifeline. I explained that I was a Fulbrighter, a quasi-employee of the US government, but it didn't seem to make all that much difference. He explained that the outlook was not good because in his experience with accidents of this kind the driver was held in prison until the trial and usually given a jail sentence. He was very matter of fact in delivering his opinion and not at all optimistic. Since I was going to end up in court I asked the Embassy man to recommend a lawyer. "Hmmm, Mr. Salimbene, we can't do that because in the past we have recommended a lawyer and the client was not happy when he was sent to jail. He blamed the Embassy." I explained I had no choice in the matter. I knew no one in Istanbul. I needed a lawyer and surely they must have worked with some lawyers that they could recommend. He hemmed and hawed and said that he did have a list of lawyers which he proceeded to produce with the flair of a magician. There were about fifty names on the list. I chose the first one and he hesitated and said, "Well, we haven't worked with him and I really can't recommend him. But I don't want to influence you in any way." I went to the second one and he repeated his stock phrase. I got to the 12th name on the list and he exhaled and said, "Well....., we know this man and we have worked with him in the past. Mind you, I am not recommending him, but he is good."

At my request the Embassy man called the lawyer and within a half hour the adventure continued with a new character added to the cast. The lawyer was greasy, fat and jovial. The first words out of his mouth were: "I love the American people!" I had an uneasy feeling that I was in trouble. He took me aside and his second statement confirmed that I was indeed in deep trouble. "My dear man," says he, "This is a very serious matter." Pregnant pause "By the way, how much money do you have?" I went into high gear. I explained or babbled that I was a poor teacher, a Fulbrighter on a grant and we had just left Greece and it was impossible to contact anyone there for money. I was on an inspired roll: banks were closed, communications were down and everything had been locked up by the terrible Colonels in charge of the dictatorship. We were going home this very day when tragedy struck. We had spent all of our money and had only fifty dollars to get us home. At the end of this outburst I just sat there panting. "Aah," says he, "Your situation is desperate!" At that moment the Embassy man took his leave and asked me to call him the following day or have my wife call him to appraise him of my fate.

Things were happening: The lawyer explained that the police were taking me off for a sobriety test. It was almost four hours after the accident! My amazement turned to alarm when I realized that

I was expected to drive the police escort to the hospital where the test would be conducted. So, the police were willing to place their lives in the hands of a drunk driver or a suspected drunk driver. I was escorted by two policeman who immediately made themselves at home in my car by turning on the radio and fiddling around with the wipers and the signals. I imagined their conversation to run along these lines, "Hey, Akmed, this little Bug has a 1500 cc engine with a clock and a radio!" "You are right Mustapha, let's get this dude to open her up once we get away from the station house." They were like two kids with a new toy and, as a result, directions were very casual and I was doing last minute turns or being forced to reverse into oncoming traffic to make the turn. They were smoking and acting like they were on a holiday. By the time we got to the hospital I was a nervous wreck and ready for a bed in the psychiatric wing. We went into the hospital with an official rush. They poked their heads into one office and barked at a doctor who came out and growled at me, "Deutsch?" "Nein" I growled back. In another office the doctor called out "Francaise?" I shrugged my shoulders with Gallic aplomb and said "Non". After that the policeman indicated that we were to go back to the car.

When we got back to the station the lawyer rushed up and told me that I was very lucky. With awe he informed me that the public prosecutor was not going to leave his office for his weekend vacation. He was going to wait to hear my case. "Great, he is giving up an early start for his weekend retreat to sentence me to life imprisonment. How kind!" Again we all piled into my car and I had to follow different and often conflicting instructions to get to the courthouse. Once there I was told to wait outside the room in which the hearing was to take place. I was all alone. It was after six in the evening and I sagged against the wall feeling very sorry for myself. I imagined myself to be some forlorn but romantic hero in the French Resistance about to face certain death or torture. Leaning against the wall all I needed was for someone to offer me the last cigarette.

But I was a non smoker and would have to reject that customary courtesy. At that moment they called me in.

We sat in a room colored civil servant green. We were grouped around the prosecutor's table and the talking began. Of course, I didn't understand a word of what was going on. There was much smiling and the lawyer was very, very deferential to the prosecutor. We were in the presence of raw power and for the first time in my life I was truly afraid. These people had the power of life and death over me. I could be sent to prison and not even the Embassy of the United States of America could do a thing about it! There was no appeal. In the eyes of their law I was a criminal and the law was harsh and unforgiving. Guilty until proven innocent. The lawyer leaned over and said the result of the sobriety test was negative. What sobriety test was that I thought, 'Nein' and 'Non'? They agree that you were not drunk, he continued to whisper, but they do not believe your story. Sotto voce I insisted that it happened just as I had explained.

There was more discussion and at some point tea was brought in. After an intense and heated debate the lawyer, clearly astonished at the Prosecutor's perspicuity, declared that the Prosecutor wanted to go to the scene of the accident to see for himself. Again I was forced to drive and my passengers were none other than our highly revered prosecutor, my lawyer and a policeman. We arrived at the scene of the accident almost at dusk, got out of the car and the lawyer was glum. Shaking his head he said, "He doesn't believe you." Just at that moment a bus pulled in and in desperation I shouted, "This is the way it happened!" and I rushed out in front of the parked bus only to be pulled back by the prosecutor himself. It was obvious to everyone what my fate would have been if I had popped out from in front of the bus as cars zoomed by nearly grazing the side of the bus. There were smiles as they tried to calm me down. I was twitching. If the prosecutor hadn't grabbed me there would not have been much left of me to prosecute.

We drove back to the courthouse and I thought I detected a note of gaiety amongst my passengers. The lawyer seemed to be agreeing with everything that the Prosecutor had to say. Back in the office the lawyer leaned over and said, "The prosecutor believes you." For the first time in eight hours I felt some of the tension ease out of my body and I sat back and crossed my legs. The lawyer lurched over from his chair and uncrossed my legs. He hissed, "We do not cross our legs in front of the public prosecutor!" All right, I thought, we do not want to lose the case after all of this due to ignorance of some cultural nuances. No, problem! Feet stay flat on the floor and we do not relax until we are back in dear old Thessaloniki. The prosecutor started dictating to a stenographer. Again the lawyer leaned over and whispered, "You owe me your life. He has found you free of all criminal negligence." Back in the world of practical issues, I whispered, "Say, how much do I owe you?" He whispered back , "A thousand dollars." "A thousand dollars!" I gasped and went into my previous litany, "But I am a poor Fulbrighter, fifty dollars left to my name, assets blocked in Greece, no one in America." He patted my hand. "You misunderstood me. I said that you could not even pay me with a thousand dollars because I have saved your life." With rising panic I squeaked, "How much do you want?" He fixed me with a look and said, "Whatever you wish to pay me." Oh, happy day. Thank you, Lord, thank you. I knew I was home free, because this had been the bargaining refrain we had heard whenever we were in the covered bazaar haggling over coveted goods. I knew whatever I offered he would double it. It was better to start off low and then he could double or triple it. But this was not the place to start haggling especially when the prosecutor was in full flight dictating my freedom.

When the document was finished and stamped and signed, we shook hands all around. The lawyer informed me that the courteous thing to do was to drive the prosecutor home since he had delayed his trip to the country for my sake. Driving at night in

Istanbul was the last thing that I wanted to do but I had so much adrenaline flowing in my system that I indicated that it was no problem and that I was aware of the peculiar honor that I had been accorded. Of course, I immediately turned into a one way street the wrong way and to the accompaniment of flashing headlights and blaring horns and imprecations to Allah, I manage do a U-turn and head off in the right direction. Everyone in the car was quite merry and thought it was a wonderful joke and my back was roundly patted. We dropped the prosecutor off at his home and I drove the lawyer to our hotel where Jane and Suzanne were anxiously waiting. In the comfort of my car I again asked him what his fee was and again he said, "Whatever you wish." I said, "I don't know what is reasonable. I am a poor teacher and you said you were a teacher once......forty dollars?" "A hundred" said he. "Done!" said I. A bright idea struck me. I had cashed in almost all of our dollars for lira at the rate of 12 to 1. If I paid him in black market lira it would cost me approximately forty dollars instead of one hundred. I asked him if he would take lira. He seemed a little taken aback but said that it was fine. He enquired if I had a hundred dollars? I said "No problem!" and produced the roll of a thousand dollars that Jane had slipped to me before I had gone to the court house, completely forgetting that I had told him that we had less then a hundred dollars to get home. He took the money with a smile and said that I should be aware that though I was exonerated from any criminal guilt I needed to be aware that a civil suit could arise and if he were in my place he would get out of town tonight. With that he bade me good night and walked off. Only later did I realize that his smile was a sign of his appreciation and recognition that he had had a worthy opponent. Obviously I had not been as stupid and naive as he had thought.

High on adrenaline I rushed up to the hotel room and told the girls to pack. We were getting out of town tonight. Jane reminded me that it was ten o'clock and we had to call the consular officer to let him know how I had fared. I called him up and told him that I was free but I was planning to leave town because I did not want to get involved in a civil suit. I was insured and would want the family to be compensated for his death but I did not want to hang around or languish in prison until the details were worked out. He said that it might not be a bad idea to change hotels, not that he was recommending this as a course of action, but it would be effective because he wanted to see me in the morning. He informed me that a certain gentleman by the name of Amir Akmet had passed by the Embassy requesting the payment of $5.00 owed to him by me. Baffled I explained that I didn't know a soul in Istanbul let alone Mr. Akmet. The embassy man explained that he understood my surprise but it turned out that Mr. Akmet was the cab driver who had driven the injured man to the hospital. Contrary to what the police had told me, he wasn't dead. Anyway the family of the injured man refused to pay the fare so he went to the U.S. Embassy to see if the driver of the vehicle that hit the injured man would pay him.

He was paid by the Embassy and promptly went to the police station to give a statement on my behalf that it had been impossible for me to avoid colliding with the victim since his actions were totally irresponsible and bordering on suicidal. So, it was with a little help from unknown friends that I had avoided a Turkish court case and incarceration. We changed hotels and the next morning went to the Embassy to pay the five dollars for the taxi cab driver. Our plans for the grand tour of Turkey were cut short. I wanted to get back to Greece in the shortest time possible, not feeling safe until I was over the border with my back to the crescent flag.

After two years with Fulbright we had to consider our future plans since a third year was not allowed. I had applied to the University of Cairo and to one of the oil companies in Saudi Arabia. Saudi replied and their literature explained how we would live in walled compounds and the restrictions placed on women. That was a non starter because Suzanne would never tolerate not driving and going around covered from head to toe. The other complication would be the fact that she was Jewish. She was actually Jewish in name only, but we were sure that the Arabs would not take into consideration "in name only". And then the "Six Days War" broke out between Israel and its neighbors. Suddenly the grantees chosen for that year began to cancel concerned that Greece might be in the middle of the action! I am sure that the average American's ignorance of Middle Eastern geography had a lot to do in influencing their decisions. The Fulbright Director came to me and asked me if I would be willing to stay on for a third year. I readily agreed and we enjoyed a third year with Fulbright and the University of Thessaloniki.

THE COLLEGE

AT THE CONCLUSION OF THE THIRD YEAR we were desperate to remain. There was an American sponsored College in Athens. It was a girls school, seventh to 12th grade, with a small undergraduate college that was more along the lines of a finishing school. They were looking for a head of the English department and I applied. I was interviewed by the principal a frail American lady who had married a Greek gentleman who had somewhere along the way passed away, bequeathing his name. To her credit she spoke Greek fluently. She smoked the strong aromatic cigarettes that the Greeks loved and gasped for breath in between puffs. Bird like in her mannerisms she informed me that the job was mine if the Vice President approved her decision. My Fulbright record and my professed love for Greece seemed to weigh heavily in my favor. She informed me that the recent head had resigned but I could meet with him and he would fill me in. It never happened. Due to departmental squabbles and machinations he had declared a pox on their house and not only left the school but the country.

I next met the Vice President a very savvy Greek who got his Ph.D. in the States along with an American wife. He was an economist and had a business background. He smoked little cheroots and kept a bottle of Johnny Walker Black Label in his desk drawer, but I learned that later and don't want to get ahead of my story. After a brief interview he declared that I was eminently suited for the job and he looked forward to working with me. I found him charming and extremely intelligent, obviously, he had hired me. But he made a great first impression. He was a Greek who understood and had an appreciation for American and Greek culture and where the conflicts lie.

The College had been founded in Turkey by American missionaries. Around the time of the catastrophe in Asia Minor things went terribly wrong. In 1914 the Turks engaged in ethnic cleansing and massacred and expelled the surviving Greeks who had been living in southern Turkey (Anatolia) from time immemorial. The refugees ended up in Thessaloniki and Athens effectively doubling the populations of those two cities. The missionaries in some cases came along with the refugees. Initially the missionaries had gone out to convert the Turks. However the only ones who showed any interest in their schools and hospitals were the Greeks who were already Christians. Once reestablished in Thessaloniki and Athens the missionaries continued their activities but the Greek authorities frowned on their proselytizing. After all, Greeks were already Christians, Greek Orthodox Christians.

The president of the College was the last appointee of the missionary board of trustees. She had a silent husband and an alcoholic daughter who liked Greek men. The daughter had a young son who wandered around our campus and I never could figure out where and if he attended school. The College was a girls school, so I knew that he wasn't with us. I had one contact with the daughter and apropos of nothing she remarked on the fact that I had a pronounced overbite. I wondered if this was some sort of dental foreplay that she was conducting given her reputation, but she promptly left my office after her pronouncement. They, mother and son disappeared after my first year.

By the time I arrived on the scene the missionaries had departed from the board of trustees and it was secular in make up. This board was no longer interested in spreading the word of the gospel. They were more interested in making the college economically independent and further developing and utilizing the very modern facilities that had been built gratis by the United States government.

The board was now composed of Greek American business men and a small number of Boston Brahmans who brought the ethos of "old money." They were generous and serious in their interest in the College. The Greek American contingent was generous to a point but they enjoyed the yearly trip back to the fatherland and the entertainment that the VP laid on when they were in town.

Initially the VP was indispensable to me. I enjoyed his support when I had to fire a couple of teachers who insisted on making the girls translate every word from English into Greek and back again. They also insisted on teaching the girls Greek expressions which had no meaning in English. For example: "They will eat you like a cauliflower." or "Are we talking about hair?" Introducing new books, methodology, and a language lab all met with resistance until I would appeal to the VP and then, like the Godfather, he would make an offer that recalcitrant teachers could not refuse. Usually, during the summer on the last day, he would schedule a meeting after school when everyone had left the building for the summer vacation. The teacher who was to be fired would be informed that her job was terminated and told to clean out her desk. In the fall a new teacher would be in place. It was tough but the VP insisted that it was part of the 'Greek reality'. This was a euphemism for how things worked or didn't work in Greece.

Some of my Greek colleagues were a little skeptical of me because I was so young and also a male in a girls school. It didn't bother me. I was brought in to modernize the department and make some changes. In addition to pedagogical differences there was also a "language divide' between the teachers who spoke 'American' English and those who spoke 'British' English. The latter believed that they were superior in every way. Looking back I probably was not a terribly successful administrator because I was inexperienced. I was from the John Wayne School of Management. Everyone should do what I said because I was the 'leader'. I learned over the years that it is not that simple. A good leader has to be a good follower and very often leadership is just the art of doing that which is possible at the time. I blush to think of my mistakes.

In attempting to effect changes I ran into the 'Greek reality' at almost every turn. The curriculum was set by the Greek Ministry of Education and Religion. Every time we attempted to introduce something new we were met with the response that the Ministry would not allow it or that there was no time for such frivolities. The pedagogy was straight out of the 19th century German tradition: memorize and repeat. The students had 12 or 13 subjects including religion, Modern Greek, Ancient Greek, and Katherevousa which was a form of High Greek used in the courts, government documents and one or two newspapers. At the College we had a retired teacher who was fluent in Katherevousa. His only job was to see that our communications with the Ministry were written properly. Anything at the time that required the governmental bureaucracy was in Katherevousa, for example, when you applied for a resident's permit there was a scribe outside of the Aliens Office who would fill out your form in the proper script and supply the ever present required government stamps. All official documents required these tax stamps.

The Greek faculty was split into three or four separate groups based on politics or personalities. Faculty meetings were horrendous. Everyone had to express an opinion even if there was no disagreement, which was rare. Then at the next meeting they would argue over the minutes. It became so bad at one point that the Greek principal brought in a tape recorder and threatened to use it because he couldn't find anyone to take minutes because who ever recorded the minutes was attacked, leading to more arguments and a constant rewriting of the minutes. The tape recorder scared the hell out of everyone and the faculty eased up and agreed to have a teacher take the minutes without interference.

At this point in time the United States was no longer very popular because it supported a coup d'état by the army colonels. The faculty was divided into a small right wing which supported the colonels and a larger left-wing which was against. It was not a happy situation. The irony was that our teachers hostile to the colonels were employed and paid by an American school. To make matters worse, it was a private school but the teachers actually had civil servant status. Of course, they were paid better than the state teachers and their teaching conditions were far superior. However, when the state teachers struck they would go out on strike with them in sympathy.

At this time a new president came in. He was a very experienced and qualified and had served as president of a U.S. college. Unfortunately, he did not have a clue about Greece nor did he speak Greek. No one had explained to him the 'Greek Reality'. He was very dependent upon the VP and to a certain degree initially very naïve. The VP did not support him. Unfortunately, the VP had a history of trying to persuade the board to make him president, but it never worked out. Blinded by his own ambition, he had been instrumental in deposing a couple of presidents but had never been successful in convincing the board to give him the top spot. He could have been a perfect number two but he wanted the top spot and thought that the new man would be a push over. To complicate matters at this point the VP was having an affair with his young secretary and he began to turn against the people, like myself and others, who had always supported him and believed in his abilities.

Several of us tried to worn the president that the VP was out to 'depose' him for want of a better word. But the president wouldn't hear of it, believing that we were over exaggerating some of the VP's failings. He valued the VP for his facility with the language and his different connections with the media and politicians and he was aware that the VP had kept the school afloat during a critical financial period. The President couldn't believe that anyone could be so distrustful or disloyal.

The President was finally convinced of the VP's duplicity one night when a group of us had gone out to dinner. It included several administrators and their wives. The dinner was in honor of a major benefactor to the college. The man was a very successful and wealthy Greek American who had made a substantial donation to the college. We were at table and the VP started to tell the benefactor a story about how badly he was being treated by the president which, of course, was an outright lie. Unfortunately, the man was advanced in age and very hard of hearing. The VP was shouting above the noise and the music that was being played. He was totally unaware that the President could overhear his blatant betrayal. Early the next morning the President called me into his office and told me that he would ask the VP to resign. It was not without sadness that we saw him go but he had been his own worst enemy. Victim of an ancient but deadly modern sin, 'hubris', overweening pride. Later the president appointed me assistant to the President and principal of the high school and that was the start of a strong mentoring relationship. Much of my success in later years I attribute to working alongside of him. He is a man of great integrity and wisdom and the College flourished under his leadership..

During one period when a strike was called, the President decided that though the teachers were going on strike, we should conduct business as usual and offer classes. The idea was that we would show films and have some sports activities. Thus we would show the parents, who paid tuition, that we were attempting to meet our responsibilities to the students. While we were planning all of this the students marched out in support of the teachers! We let them go and the president and I learned a precious lesson. When it came to politics we were rank amateurs. An appeal to reason that they were better paid then their public school colleagues and therefore there was no reason to make our students suffer had no influence on the teachers. In future whenever they struck, salaries were withheld and that kept them in check.

On another occasion the girls walked out in protest over some issue and locked themselves in the gym. The Greek principal and I went in to meet with them and got them back to class with the promise to meet with their leadership. We met in my office with the Greek principal, the dean of students and a couple of other teachers. When they filed in I realized that I was in trouble because they (the adults) had moved their chairs in a way in which they were sitting with the students and everyone was facing me. There I was, the 'hated' American and my colleagues with whom I had broken bread, attended weddings, and funerals, and considered to be friends were now allied against me. Well, I took my lumps and in the end the girls left feeling empowered. My colleagues came up to me and told me that I had handled it superbly, etc., etc. It was like the last scene in High Noon, but in my rendition I didn't say or do anything. They were a little chastened because they realized what they had done. The Greek principal was especially nervous because he and I were very close and I had convinced the president at one point to rehire him although he had once been fired from the top spot. He realized how angry I was and he was waiting for me to round on him and call him every name under the sun, but I held my tongue and did not say a word.

At the end of the day I went home. I scared myself by the level of anger I felt. I wanted to smash and throttle 'my friend'. For the first time in my life I was truly enraged. I was angry, but why? What was I really feeling? It took me a couple of days in which I avoided him and tried to puzzle it all out. I finally realized that I was angry because I was hurt. I felt betrayed. I had to look up the word in the Greek dictionary, I had never had to use it before. This man was my friend and he betrayed me. The next morning I called him in to my office and he started to apologize and I asked him to wait and hear me out. I told him what I was feeling and as I started to talk to him tears came to my eyes and I started to cry. The effect was startling. He expected me to attack him and here I was crying because I felt betrayed. I couldn't have inflicted a greater punishment on him if I had hit him with a baseball bat. John Wayne would not have handled it that way, but it saved our friendship. This experience taught me a lesson, stop and think about what you are really feeling before you shoot your mouth off or write a memo.

They were good years and I learned a lot but there were many frustrations. However, I was in love with the country and the life style. There was a constant feeling of an adventure just being around the corner. We traveled to different places, Thailand, Singapore, Egypt, Turkey, England, India, Israel and Tunisia. But it was also that sense that no two days were ever alike in Greece. One day I got a call from the Dean saying that the cleaning woman had found a bomb in one of the corridors. I thought it was an overreaction to someone finding an unidentified school bag. I went by the office of the head of building and grounds and jokingly told him to come along with me because they had found a bomb upstairs. He was a former Colonel in the Greek Marines and he was a screamer. He had a good heart but he treated us all like we were dim privates. We went up and just as we got to the Greek principal's office one of the Greek teachers came out with a very serious expression. He said that it was a bomb. He had very courageously taken it from the cleaning woman and walked it out on to a patch of waste ground far from the classrooms and the kids. The cleaning woman had brought it to the principal thinking that the plastic bag she found on the corridor door was some kid's sneakers. The Dean saw it and she told the teacher who had dropped by her office at that very moment. The teacher didn't hesitate. He recognized it for what it was, picked it up and took it away so the children were not in any danger. We later learned that the bomb had had a faulty timer and had been set to go off on the weekend when no one was in the building. Unfortunately, none of the girls used the corridor where the bomb had been placed. It was resting on a door handle. An anti-American group that had been planting bombs around Athens had left the bomb. We were shocked because we always relied on the belief that Greeks loved and cherished children and that terrorists would never endanger their lives.

We were all shaken. The colonel went out to the waste ground to take a look at the bomb. I didn't because I felt there was no reason to go near it and take a risk since the kids were safe and why be possibly maimed or killed for the sake of curiosity. I thought about it later and realized how precious life was and how foolhardy it was to risk it for no reason. I like to think that if the teacher had not walked the bomb out or had not been there I would have done it because the children had to be protected and that was my job. Fortunately for the children and me I was never put to that test.

GREEN EYES

WHEN WE ARRIVED IN GREECE we were given several orientations by U.S. government representatives. One that had an impact on me was given by the Air Force Base doctor. We had been told all sorts of stories about not eating fresh vegetables and that everything bought in the markets should be washed in chlorine or a green disinfectant that was locally available. The doctor told us that was nonsense because Greek farmers didn't use 'night soil', human waste, to fertilize their crops. He told us to enjoy the fruits and vegetables because very little fertilizer of any kind was used. The only advice that he could give us was to avoid shell fish at all costs because quite often they were taken from inside harbors where waste material often flowed and it was an unnecessary risk for hepatitis. We followed that rule throughout our stay. It wasn't a problem because I didn't care for shellfish and was never tempted.

This sets the stage for my story. One weekend I went to Piraeus with a group of friends. Our objective was to visit a taverna that served only ouzo and side dishes that went with it (meze). Ouzo is the anise flavored drink that is made from the mash that is left after the wine is extracted. Ouzo is the equivalent of American 'white lightening'. It is an extremely powerful aperitif and one never drinks it without having something to eat. Usually it is served before the meal to stimulate the appetite. This taverna or 'ouzerie' as the Greeks called it, had the reputation for serving over one hundred mezes and no one had ever been able to actually complete the one hundred offerings or start a second round. The group that I was with had a mission to accomplish. We intended to go through the entire menu. With each round of ouzo that we ordered came a

65

new meze. On that night we completed our mission. There was no banner to herald "Mission Accomplished" as we staggered out, but we felt like true Olympians. Someone suggested it would be a smart idea to have dinner before we set out for home. It would give us some time to steady ourselves for the drive back to Athens. We went to the harbor and had dinner and on one of the last plates was an raw oyster. Someone suggested that I finish it off and despite the doctor's warning I popped it into my mouth. That oyster was my undoing.

The following day I had a terrible headache and I called our local doctor who was a fine physician of the old school. Just by looking at you he seemed to be able to diagnose your complaint and he made house calls. Even though he spoke no English I trusted him completely. I called him and he came over. He looked at me and I could tell that he saw something, but he just said that the headache had nothing to do with my head. It was my stomach that was causing the pain. That seemed reasonable after the antics of the night before and the copious amounts of ouzo that I had consumed. The next day I went to school and by midday I was completely wiped out. I went into the restroom and looked in the mirror and discovered that my eyes were yellow. I decided to go home.

I called the doctor and told him that I was feeling very tired and that my eyes had turned 'green'. The conversation was in Greek and I had mixed up my colors. He said, "Impossible!" I clarified the mistake and said 'yellow'. He asked me if my urine was the color of cognac and I said that it was. He said, "You are a very sick man. You must go to the hospital immediately." "What do I have?", I queried. "You have ipatitita!", he said. "What's that?", I asked. "I don't know English!", he replied in exasperation. Then it dawned on me, 'ipatitita'…..'hepatitis'. "Do you mean hepatitis? I queried. "I don't know English. You are a very sick man. You have to go to the hospital." He came over to the house and asked me what hospital I wanted to go to. I wanted to avoid going to the hospital at all costs.

Although health care was free and the doctors excellent the conditions in the hospitals were very basic. I had friends who had been hospitalized. The food was often inedible and the basic comforts were totally lacking, you had to bring their own toilet paper. The nursing care was very limited and you needed to have family or a friend stay over to help you go to the bathroom or bathe. The wards were noisy filled with family members taking care of their kin. It seemed that the visiting hours were not restricted at all. The one good thing was that they allowed a family member or a friend to stay over to help the patient.

I told him that at all costs I wanted to avoid the hospital and since the therapy was bed rest why couldn't I do that at home? He said that I would need a vitamin B shot everyday and did I know a nurse. I asked him to recommend one. He said that he knew a very competent one and he would make the arrangements. He instructed Suzanne to go out and purchase 24 syringes and the ampoules of vitamin B. He told us the nurse used reusable needles which would not be a good idea in my case. We couldn't believe that you could just go to the pharmacy and buy the needles. He explained that there was no problem and it wasn't against the law. As a matter of fact we learned that you could purchase any drug at the pharmacy without prescription if you knew the name and the dose.

The doctor informed us that the nurse would come bright and early the next day to give me my shot. At eight o'clock in the morning I heard this awful racket. A motor bike was under our window and it seemed that the throttle was stuck at full blast. Suzanne looked out the window and described a tiny, wisp of a lady in goggles and helmet who was carrying a black medical satchel. My nurse had arrived. Suzanne let her in and she blew into the bedroom like a tiny tornado. She was from Crete and we couldn't understand a word she was saying. With the flare of a magician she opened her black bag and revealed an array of metal syringes with needles in place. We quickly indicated that we had the syringes and we didn't need any of hers. She was a little dismissive of the plastic syringes but agreed to use them. Over the course of twenty four days she administered 24 shots and I never felt a thing. She was an angel, an angel on a motorbike.

YELLOW JOURNALISM

AT THIS TIME IN GREECE there must have been about a dozen newspapers in Athens. One for every political party. Though Athens was the cosmopolitan capitol of the country these newspapers would make the Enquirer look like Pulitzer prize material. There were a few good ones but they are not the ones that concern this narrative. The first headline story involved the College. The Dean had invited an American psychologist to join the faculty and teach among other courses one on Human Sexuality. The instructor had been alerted to the conservative of the conservative nature of Greek society and had chosen a book that was considered conservative and not at all provocative by American standards. There were no photos just some drawings of the human anatomy and positions involved in intercourse. The course. The course was extremely popular and not at all controversial thanks to the professionalism and teaching ability of the instructor.

However, a dissatisfied employee of the college brought the course to the attention of the leftwing press by showing them a drawing of a man and woman purportedly engaged in rear entry intercourse. They were led to believe that the College was promoting the insidious "Turkish custom" of anal intercourse! The papers charged that the Americans were once again corrupting Greek youth, and highlighting the dangers of having American sponsored education in Greece. Within hours we were informed that the Ministry of Education was sending an inspector to examine these charges and obviously to punish the wrong doers. Our position in Greek education was always being challenged for one reason or another, but now there was something serious allegedly threatening the very foundations of Greek morality!

The president allowed me to lead on this matter and I met with the inspector and the instructor who had never dreamt that he would be making headlines in a number of the Athenian papers. The inspector started off with the usual questions concerning the instructor's name, father's name, mother's name and then achingly meticulously asked questions about the course. It was a tedious process that took hours. But in the course of the questioning the inspector, to his credit, began to understand the value of the course and the fact that we were not attempting to subvert the morals of Greek youth. At one point we learned that the young wife of one of the members of parliament was taking the course and she in a fury asked her husband to help us fend off the lies and exaggerations that some of the papers were spreading. Once more the value of friends paid off. Once the papers had milked the issue for everything it was worth the inspector confessed that he wished he had had the benefit of this course when he was a young man. The College was not closed down, but we were advised, that though it was an excellent course we should not offer it in future. After the firestorm of controversy and the weeks of upset we took the inspector's friendly advice and the course was never offered again.

There was another scandal which did not have a happy ending. At one of the private schools a Cypriot history teacher with a Ph.D. challenged his students to not react to clichés but to dig deep and get the facts, to understand where your adversary was coming from in any argument. He challenged them to study the Turkish point of view on the Cyprus situation. Cyprus had been invaded by Turkey and occupied half of the island. The second part of the assignment was now that the students had the facts and knew their adversaries' arguments, they could counter and intelligently argue the cause of the Greek Cypriots. Unfortunately the students never got to the second part of the assignment because, again a dissatisfied employee went to the papers and declared that this American school was indoctrinating Greek youth against their own country. Headlines screamed out damning the nefarious American educational system. The irony was that the headmaster of the school was an Englishman who was a true philhellene and he was married to a Cypriot woman. To think that anyone in this case would have gone against the interests of Greece was laughable. Unfortunately, the case took a nasty twist when the Ministry of Education sent out an inspector to obtain statements and find out what was going on.

Again teacher and students were interviewed and interrogated and meticulous notes were taken. The inspector happened to visit the library and the librarian innocently showed him where the students did research and in the course of looking through some files he came across pamphlets that the students had gotten from the Turkish Embassy when they were researching information for the Model United Nations. Normally the information would have been thrown out after the students had finished the project but the librarian had not got around to weeding out the file. For the inspector he had found the "smoking gun"! The school was libeled in the press and condemned but it was obvious that the story was being controlled, because it was widely known that the American ambassador's son was studying at the school and the papers would have had a field day with this information but it never came to light. Tragically as a result the headmaster, the librarian and the teacher lost their jobs. The headmaster was informed that he would never be allowed to work in Greece ever again. He and his family were forced to leave the country. The teacher and his wife went back to Cyprus.

THE POLICE COME CALLING

ONE AFTERNOON SUZANNE CALLED ME IN GREAT DISTRESS. She said that four plainclothes policeman had barged into the house when they rang and she opened the door. They were searching the house looking under the beds and in the closets. They went into the basement where I had set up a darkroom. I have always been a keen amateur photographer. While in the basement they came across my tools that I used for household repairs. They found all of this very suspicious and kept asking her why I had the tools and what was I photographing? I tried to calm her down and told her to put one of the policemen on the phone. Now it must be remembered that despite taking lessons my Greek wasn't fluent at this time so I tried to keep the conversation simple:

Me: What are you doing in my house?

Policeman: This is just a routine search.

Me: Why have you chosen my house?

Policeman: A car was stolen and someone reported that the thief went into your house. That is why we are here.

I went on to tell him that he didn't have the right to search my house without my permission. That was foolish on my part because they could do whatever they damn pleased since the Colonels were in power. I asked for the address of their police station and he told me where they were based. I asked him to stop frightening my wife and I would go to the station to answer any questions that they had.

I went to the VP's office and told him what had happened. He assured me that there was nothing to be afraid of and it was probably a mistake. He suggested that I should go to the police station alone and find out what was going on. I didn't share his view of things because I had heard stories and knew people who had seen relatives locked up without any due process. There was also the punishment of exile where people were sent for an indefinite time to an island and not allowed to travel off the island. I was extremely nervous.

I went home first to see how Suzanne was doing and she said at one point though she was frightened, they were like the Keystone Cops tripping over themselves and seeming to spend a lot of time arguing amongst themselves. I told her that I was going to the police station and if I wasn't back in a couple of hours to call the VP. With sweaty palms, and pounding heart, I arrived at the police station. Before I could state my business they demanded to know my name, my mother's maiden name, and my father's name which was George. It was unusual for a son to bear the same name as the father. The child was usually named after a grandparent. I presented my resident's permit and my passport. When I was allowed to explain the nature of my business, I was told to stop. I had to go upstairs to the security police. This sent a chill down my spine.

I climbed a rickety staircase and came into a small room that had a naked light bulb hanging from the ceiling. There was a young fellow sitting at a beat up desk. He was in civilian clothes with his shirtsleeves rolled up above his elbows. He had long hair and wore tight black pants and pointy shoes. He looked like one of the boys who hung out in the tourist spots trying to pick up foreign girls. For obvious reasons these fellows were called "harpoons". Before I could get in a word edgewise he wanted to know my name, father's name, etc., etc. All of this information was taken down on a date pad for Champion Spark plugs. It didn't appear to be terribly official but that was the least of my worries. At this point I was wondering if I should have called the school lawyer instead of listening to the VP. The young man explained that I had to wait for the officer in charge to come in. He informed me that the officer was on serious business at that moment. I took a seat wondering which island

I was going to be sent to. Finally the officer came in adjusting his uniform and from his puffy face I realized that the 'serious business' had been the afternoon siesta.

The "harpoon" surrendered his seat at the desk and mumbled a few words to the officer. The officer studied the slip of paper and repeated the questions word for word that I had twice before been obliged to divulge. He wanted to know what my problem was. While waiting for him I had worked out my strategy. I explained that I was a friend of Greece and had come to the country on a scholarship from the U.S. government. I knew that there were a lot of bad things in the press about Greece but I was a staunch supporter of my 'adopted' country. If at any time the police wanted to come to my house I had no problem with that. I would welcome them, but the men who had come to my house had forced their way in and had frightened my wife.

He responded with the story about the stolen car and I agreed that that was reasonable grounds for suspicion but certainly not to frighten an innocent woman. He agreed with me and turned to the "harpoon" and said that he would have to punish the men who had gone to the foreigner's house. The exaggerated manner in which he said this left me in no doubt that nothing would come of it, but more importantly I wouldn't be heading out to lonely exile. What had caused this incident? A week earlier a bomb had been exploded near the U.S. Embassy. The culprits had not been found. At this time we were engaged in finding apartments and furnishings for the new teachers who had come into Greece. We had different faculty staying with us and cars and trucks bearing furniture came and went from our doorstep. I later learned that in our small neighborhood the comings and goings of the new teachers had raised suspicions about us. Obviously someone in the neighborhood reported this 'suspicious' activity and that resulted in the raid. We were never troubled again but at the time it was frightening.

MOUNT ATHOS

ADVENTURE WAS NEVER FAR OFF AND ONE EASTER I traveled back to Thessaloniki with my good friend Dave Harris, a former Fulbrighter and professor at Georgetown University. We were going to Mt. Athos to visit the monasteries located on a peninsula five hours north of the city No women were allowed on the Holy Mountain even though it was dedicated to the Virgin Mary! Before visiting you had to get a visa from the Ministry of Education and Religion in Athens. Once that was done it was like traveling to a foreign country. We stayed overnight at the Electra Palace Hotel, a new luxury class hotel at that time, had dinner at the Olympus Naousa restaurant, long gone, and picked up our bus tickets.

The Monastery of Philothei

After a good night's sleep we were up at 4:45 a.m. to get over to the EKTEL bus line. Traveling at that time in Greece was always a great adventure: Would the bus leave? Would there be a bus? Would it leave on time? Would it be going in the right direction? It actually left on time, stranding two German tourists who had wandered off to buy some breakfast. We left Thessaloniki in a haze of diesel fumes and headed northeast. The countryside was coming into bloom and it was achingly green.

Everyone started eating after we left the city behind. This made me nervous because the Greeks tended to be bad travelers and were usually sick to their stomachs whether on a bus, boat or train. Sure enough, a little boy I had noticed started turning green and there was a shout from his father for a plastic bag which the conductor quickly supplied, spurred on by the reality that he would have to clean up the mess if he didn't get it into the boy's hands in time. The odor of vomit permeated the bus and everyone started opening the windows. It stopped the feeding frenzy for a little while.

After that there was more excitement when a local tough picked on two young gay boys from Athens and took their seats. After much yelling and screaming the other passengers supported the boys' rights to sit. Everyone had told us that we had to bring food because the fare at the monasteries was very bad, so Dave and I had packed our rucksacks with cans of spam, sardines and other forms of mystery meats. Despite the early hour we succumbed and opened a can of spam and made sandwiches with some packaged pumpernickel. Our adventure had begun!

Karaies

We arrived in Ouranopoulis (Heavenly City) at 10:30 a.m. and took the caique 'Miltiades' (a Greek fishing boat) to Daphni. This is where you picked up the bus to take you to Karyia the capital and where you submitted your visa. The sea fortunately was very calm and we traveled in the company of about thirty pilgrims. The trip was without incident and took us about an hour and a half. Once in Daphni we had to wait two hours for a bus to pick us up. Meanwhile a couple of other caiques came in and there were about 60 pilgrims waiting for a bus that would hold about twenty people. The tension mounted. Nothing in Greece was ever simple or without anxiety, tension and drama. The bus arrived and the driver was a tyrant who apparently had many years of experience in dealing with anxious pilgrims. He would not let anyone near the bus until all of the baggage was packed on top of the bus. Then he dramatically gave the signal for us to fight our way onto the bus. Dave and I nearly got seats but we just were not aggressive enough, so we ended up standing. There was only about a five foot four head room clearance and poor Dave's head impacted with the roof every time we hit a bump.

On the boat trip over we had met a doctor and his party of three. They had traveled from Drama. His name was Alexandros and he turned out to be the hometown choirmaster. They were looking forward to singing the liturgy in the monasteries. For them this was akin to traveling to Woodstock. He was very friendly and he spoke to us in English and eventually invited us to join his party. When speaking to us his voice would drop to low conspiratorial tones more befitting a conspiracy to knock over a bank rather than a visit to a monastery.

We went to a hotel with Alexandros and his comrades. It was called "Hotel Super Prima Good". You went through the kitchen in order to get to the backyard to mount the steps that took you up to the second floor. Dave and I got a neat two bed bedroom off the middle bedroom. The place was 'super luxury" with a sink, cold running water in the bedroom, plenty of blankets and clean sheets. What more could a man ask for? I should note that throughout the trip, all of the places we stayed were clean but just terribly ramshackle. Alexandros took us down to visit a "sketi" directed by the brother of a friend of his. A 'sketi' was a small community of monks that lived like a family. We arrived at dinner time and went into the refectory. There were about twenty monks present and one was reading while the others ate. At the head of the table sat an old wizened monk who rang a bell at one point to signify that the meal had ended. We later learned that he was the former "igoumenos" or abbot of the monastery. Alexandros' friend's brother was the new abbot. He greeted us and apologized for the meal which was a delicious cold soup with no oil or meat stock. It was just made of chick peas and herbs. But it was the best soup that I have ever eaten anywhere. It was served with fresh bread that was still hot from the oven. We felt that it was a feast. I remember the meal to this day. After dinner the new igoumenos greeted us warmly and offered us Turkish delight something that Dave and I hated and had sworn not to eat. Turkish delight is pure sugar somehow made chewy and scented with rosewater. It could throw a person into a diabetic coma from fifty yards away. But under the circumstances we manfully swallowed this cloyingly sweet concoction.

We noticed that there were a number of young monks about very subdued. If addressed they replied, but one had the impression that they were more accustomed to remaining silent. Dave and I were both struck by their disheveled appearance. Other young monks that we had seen struck Dave and I as being very effeminate looking, with their long hair done up in a pony tail. There was something very sensual about them. At one monastery I was surprised to find a Horofilakas (Police who worked in the provinces as opposed to the big cities). Surprised to find one on the Holy Mountain I enquired about his duties. I asked him if he was there to prevent the theft of holy icons and other treasures. He said the major crimes that they dealt with had to do with crimes of passion. He explained that in the sketis if a young man was lured away to a rival sketi it could have most unfortunate results. I didn't ask him to elaborate any further.

At seven-thirty that evening we went to the evening service and stayed for an hour. The ceremony is quite beautiful and the chapel was filled with shadows and the rich smell of beeswax candles. There was no electricity. The chanting removes you to another world, a world in which men have given their whole beings to God. The smell of incense and beeswax candles, the chanting, the sweeping black robes of the monks, the lined faces of the old monks and the beauty of the young ones all contributed to a feeling of magic and otherworldliness. We went to bed at about nine after tossing and turning for a long while. Procustes would have enjoyed the experience. Procrustes was the son of Posidon and would invite travelers to sleep in an iron bed that he had constructed. If they were too short he would stretch them and if they were too long for the bed he would cut them down to size.

We got up at 5:30 a.m. and found that it had rained during the night. The sky was overcast and forbidding. Alexandros and his friends started off for the Monastery Iviron much earlier than we. Dave and I took the muddy road down to the other side of the peninsula. It was rough going because the "road" was in poor condition and very soft from the previous night's rain. We hiked along for 45 minutes and then had our breakfast: cheese and bread for Dave and bread and sardines for me. Our food supply was adequate and complemented the monks' frugal meals very nicely. Here I should note that once admitted to the Holy Mountain you were guaranteed hospitality at the monastery as long as you arrived before sundown and you could stay usually a maximum of two or three nights nights. I suspect you could stay longer if you spoke Greek and were able to ingratiate yourself with the abbot or the igoumenos. We brought quite a lot of extra food, but it really wasn't necessary because what the monks gave you was very nourishing. Looking back on it I would have taken my chances with monastery fare rather than humping a heavy pack with canned goods and camera.

The Monastery of Vatopediou

The descent was pleasant despite the poor road. The sun came in and out and we were treated to many spectacular displays of flowers, cloud formations and a magnificent rainbow. We arrived at Iviron and were offered coffee and shone to our rooms. I was asked who I was and was I Orthodox, etc. Dave was considered a mystery because he is Orthodox, but speaks little Greek and is very Anglo Saxon looking. I on the other hand looked Mediterranean, spoke Greek but was a Catholic. I could have lied but I didn't want to abuse their hospitality, besides I was afraid they would ask me to pray in Greek and then I would be found out! We went to Church services for an hour and a half and then visited the refectory where they had some excellent icons and wall paintings. We went on to the library to view the old letters and vestments that they had on display there.

For lunch we had chick pea soup, but this time it was not as good as the previous night's fare. It was very watery, but tasty. We went upstairs after lunch to try and nap, but twice we were awakened by hammering and yelling before we were just about to doze off. Dave opined they were rebuilding the monastery in our honor. We finally gave up and went out to walk along the beach.

Dinner that night was bean soup with some rice. Dave and I had feasted on our hidden supplies: cheese and salami on some stolen bread. We were tired after dinner and turned in vowing not to go down to the church service, but at 11:45 the door burst open and the monk in charge of hospitality told us that the ceremony had begun. Being too much of a coward to stay in bed, I talked Dave into going down. The chanting was composed of two parts. Left and right sides of the church. There were many laymen who participated in this service. Candlelight, incense, dark shadows, seamed faces all lent it an air of mystery and romance. We went to bed at 2 a.m.

The next day we left Iviron at 10:00 a.m. after losing and then retrieving Dave's glasses from an abandoned garden. We were nervous that there would not be any room for us on the boat which was taking us to the Great Lavra Monastery. The trip to Lavra took one hour by boat and again fortune smiled on us and the sea was calm. After landing we had to climb up to the monastery which took about twenty minutes. It was grueling because the sun was strong and our packs filled with canned goods were heavy. The last part of the ascent was a sprint so that we could maintain our place in the pack and not be left behind. Sure enough once we reached the gates of the monastery we were told to wait outside. A rumor circulated that there was no room for us and we might have to find another place to stay which would mean a long hike and the fear that we would not reach safety before sundown. The thought of spending the night outside a monastery's walls was frightening, for all we knew there were wolves and all sorts of wild beasts not to mention the discomfort of sleeping rough out of doors.

Fortunately, the monks let us in and showed us to the refectory to view the wall paintings while arrangements were made to put us up for the night. I had noticed a Greek man who had traveled on the boat with us. He was dressed in climbing clothes, solid boots, knickers, long socks etc. He looked very fit and seemed to be an experienced walker. As we were looking around the refectory he threw back his head and said, "Po, Po, Po, poli oreo!" "My, My how beautiful!" And he fell down dead. We were all stunned. There was no doctor present and no one, including Dave and me, knew anything then about CPR. Initially we thought that he had fainted and there were calls to give him air. His color quickly changed to white and a monk knelt down, crossed the man's arms on his chest and simply said, "He's dead. After much consternation he was taken away. In the presence of death everyone spoke in whispers as the monks served us coffee and water. I was badly in need of the water and would have welcomed an ouzo.

Easter Sunday Procession

The monks at Lavra were very friendly and the gate keeper told us that the procession with the holy icon was about to take place and that we should be ready to take pictures. Although still stunned by the sudden death of one of the pilgrims what followed was an orgy of picture taking. It was a very colorful scene with the chanting monks carrying the silver and gold icon and waving censors. The chanting and the aroma of incense all lent an air of mystery and deep faith. After the procession around the property of the monastery we were taken to the refectory again and this time fed at double time. We were all knocked out, but we had not been assigned rooms. We were worried and so was the monk who was in charge. He was extremely friendly and courteous but rather fretful at the large number of pilgrims. At that point rumors began to surface again: no room, too many pilgrims! Finally, we all emitted a great sigh of relief when they showed us to our rooms. At that point we teamed up with the boys who had had been given a hard time on the bus. They knew the monk in charge and had heard that only one room had mattresses. We got the one room, but later we learned that the other rooms had mattresses and no one had to sleep on the floor. After getting settled Dave and I walked around taking pictures and looking at the frescoes that adorned the walls.

The next day lunch was a weak soup of macaroni. We thanked God that we did not get beans again. It is all very good to be walking in the open air after consuming bean soup, but closed in a small room could be deadly. A walk up behind the monastery wasn't too interesting because the vegetation was very dense but we took the advantage of using nature's facilities because the monastery toilets were just horrific, centuries of use created an odor that was akin to poison gas. When we returned to the monastery more visitors had arrived and they were forced to find whatever shelter was available. At dinner time we didn't get a place in the dining room so we went with one of the boys who had in the meantime changed their quarters and were now ensconced in a nice room in a newly refurbished section of the monastery.

At twelve o'clock we were awakened by the bells and went off to church. We lit candles and went out to the courtyard and the chanting continued and the bells were played by a monk seated at a carillon. It was beautiful. We went off to bed at 2:00 a.m.

We awoke at 7:00 a.m. Alcohol baths and an ice-cold face wash got us ready for the new day. The Easter feast was served at 8:00 a.m.: macaroni soup, lamb, and wine. We met up with some other Fulbrighters and compared notes. No one could top our story about the man who was struck dead.

We went down to the quay at 9:00 a.m. and foolishly sat in the sun and shelled walnuts. We wanted to go to Aghiou Dionisiou but boats were only running in the opposite direction. The only boat that left in the morning was a small boat with the dead man wrapped in sailcloth with only his hiking boots showing. He was being taken to Daphne and then on to Thessaloniki. 12:30 arrived and still no boat. At 1:30 a boat finally arrived headed in the right direction but we had to wait an hour for a member of parliament and his party to finish up a little celebration at the police station. We were certain that they were buying icons and other treasures from the monks.

It is here that I should say something about the member of parliament. He was a most vile character. A face that revealed depravity and debauchery, very much like the face that was on the painting of Dorian Grey. We had first encountered him and his entourage at Lavra. He was accompanied by a German photographer dressed in black leather. There were three other hangers on who seemed out of place in these holy surroundings. Taken together they all looked like something straight out of a Fellini movie. They were recording and photographing like mad even though it was supposedly forbidden to take pictures inside the monastery. They appeared to be everywhere and I felt as if the place had been defiled by these characters.

Our two young gay friends tied up with the group and they all seemed to get along famously. While we waited for them to finish celebrating Easter in the police station I was fighting a bad headache that got worse when we arrived at Dioniysiou. Dave and I were the first up to the monastery. The monk in charge informed me that they didn't have enough room for everybody. This was getting to be an old story. Finally after much arguing and jostling with some German tourists we found a room in the attic of the monastery. There was a toilet with a seat, the first we had seen since coming onto the Holy Mountain.

I should say a word about an Austrian tourist, a school teacher working in Istanbul, who was constantly under foot. We wanted to strangle him after a while because he was constantly around asking questions and snapping pictures. When we first met him he had in tow a Greek boy who spoke English. I thought that the young fellow was acting as a guide interpreter but Dave thought the young Greek had been "captured" by the Austrian when the latter under-

stood that the boy spoke English. The young Greek managed at some point to slip away from his "captor". The Austrian later teamed up with three consumptive Germans who hacked and coughed and smoked cigarettes that smelled like smoldering camel dung.

It was with this foursome that we shared a room. They smoked, coughed, and barked at each other in stage whispers. When we went down to see the church we found more tour-

Our Monastery Cell ists arriving every second. By good fortune

87

we were first in line for dinner. The refectory was completely decorated with beautiful frescoes and we sat at a long refectory table.
At the head table sat the MP and his entourage. I was waiting for
a thunderbolt to smite them. In addition to our two young friends
from the bus, the entourage now included an archimandrite that
we had come across in Karyes. We were in a small shop in Karyes
when we heard this falsetto English voice exclaim "Oh, My dear,
how are you? Oh, it's unbelievable here. I've eaten nothing but
bean soup!!" With a theatrical sigh, "Oh it would be so much better
if **you** were here." We turned to find the voice coming from a tall
monk on the telephone. We didn't know what to make of it. We
thought he was an impostor, but we learned later that he was an
archimandrite, an abbot who is the head of a monastery or several
monasteries. He was from Australia and was in Greece to study the
monks' way of life and to learn Greek. Things became curiouser
and curiouser! After dinner we were caught up in a tour of the
monastery with the entourage and the Austrian who clung to us
like a limpet. At one point we broke away from the group because
we felt they belonged in a painting by Hieronymus Bosch. Chaucer
would have loved to add them to his list of pilgrims.

Once outside in the fresh air we took a long walk and met the
monk who was in charge of guarding the door and cleaning the sta-
bles. He was a great Falstaffian character who seemed to get along
well with the Germans. Outside the monastery all the Germans sat
in a row. It looked like a meeting of the Munich brewers associa-
tion. We took some pictures and then retired. Once again the beds
did not have springs. The mattresses were placed on boards and the
pillows felt like tiny cement bags. Despite all the discomfort, I slept
very well. Dave was running a fever and felt pretty uncomfortable.
At first finding that there was no room in the inn did not do our
weakened conditions much good. We were exhausted from all the
running around, the irregular hours and the anxiety of wondering

where we would be able to sleep.   But all that passed when we did find "beds" and a place for the night.

We were up early at 5:30 and ready for whatever the new day held. We were in a quandary because we knew that the crowd we were with would move on to the monastery Simon Petra and we would probably have the same noise and confusion and lack of beds. We thought of staying another day at Dionysiou and let the crowd move on, but Dave suggested that we go to Aghiou Gregoriou monastery and back track if we found that it was crowded. It seemed like a good plan. We went down to the quay to get the boat, but when it arrived it was loaded to the gunnels with pilgrims and a dozen shouting boy scouts who created mass confusion when they alighted from the boat. We decided to walk to Gregoriou which was only an hour away. The walk was mostly uphill and I was sweating profusely. We met two old men on the path and I felt sorry for them. I was absolutely sure that they wouldn't make it. Dave and I stopped for a snack on a bridge that crossed a pleasant little stream. Fifteen minutes later the two old men came huffing and puffing up to us. They were talking back and forth and made no effort to save their breath. After we finished our snack we caught up to them and passed them again. All this while we were worried that we would be met by a flock of German tourists and would again be threatened with not finding a room. When we arrived to our astonishment the two old men were chatting with one of the monks. How they had accomplished this hare and tortoise finish left us scratching our heads. Obviously there had been a short cut somewhere along the line.

We descended on Gregoriou and passed through rich arbors and fields. We met a fellow pilgrim who said that he had missed his boat. I wasn't in the mood for polite chit chat so I just asked him where we went to check in. He pointed the way and that was the last we saw of him. We entered a courtyard and were confronted by an enormous monk who told us in fractured German to go in and eat. I told him that I spoke Greek and didn't understand German. This pleased him and when I told him that I was an American he smiled and in English said "Al Capone, Chicago!" He told us to go right in because breakfast was being served. Breakfast consisted of cod fish in tomato sauce, wine bread and hard boiled, red Easter eggs. Even though we had eaten a half hour before, we ate again with gusto. I liked the fish but Dave was not crazy about it. The wine was excellent. We were light-headed by the time we left the refectory. We were then shown to our room. It was very clean with two beds, a table, a mirror and a key that actually locked the door!!! The monks of Gregoriou were extremely well organized. The toilets were clean with seats and toilet paper. There was running water in all the bowls. I should mention that part of our equipment was always a roll of toilet paper because the toilets were primitive. At one monastery I remember you had to go out on a balcony at the front of the monastery which was several hundred feet up in the air. A couple of holes had been cut into the balcony floor and with your derriere out in the wind you did your business which fell down the front of the monastery. It had been designed this way to prevent attackers from crawling up the face of the Monastery!

There were very few other tourists, two or three Greeks. The Germans all went on to the more famous monasteries, but at Gregoriou we found a peace and solitude that we had been vainly hoping to find in the other monasteries. There were open streams in the courtyard so you always had the sound of rushing water. It was magnificent. After wandering around for a few hours, we went upstairs and slept soundly for about three and a half hours. Looking back on the trip we seemed to nap frequently but we were walking around quite a bit and a most of our travels were up hill. In this case we had been exhausted by the previous day's labors. Afterwards we got up and went out to take pictures and get a better feel of the place. The monks were extremely friendly. After a dinner of hot potatoes in a tomato sauce they invited us to help them cut beans. It made us feel a part of the community. The monk who had invoked Al Capone and Chicago greeted us with a big smile and "Al Capone, Chicago".

We went to afternoon church service and then again at midnight. I went not out of obligation but because I wanted to be with the monks. I hadn't slept well because of the long afternoon nap but after attending church for two hours, I went back to sleep and did not wake up till 6 a.m. The following night we stayed up late with the monk Theodoros or "Chicago" as I nicknamed him. We were very content sitting in the courtyard listening to the frogs and the other night sounds. Dave and I both felt that we were under the spell of Gregoriou.

The next morning we regretfully took the boat back to Daphni, went through police inspection (everyone had to have his luggage searched because people were carrying away valuables), then took another boat to Ouranoupolis and a crowded bus back to Thessaloniki. It was May Day and all along the road people were marching in procession or were feasting on lamb grilled on open air pits, with crowns of flowers on their heads. We were eager to get to Thessaloniki and have a bath, a regular meal and a bed with clean sheets, but every so often the bus driver would be induced to stop beside one of the roadside parties, and half the bus would pile out and buy food. A few even joined in the dancing. Then somehow everyone would reassemble on our old bus, and away we would go again.

Thessaloniki seemed like heaven. We took baths and had a huge steak dinner with an ice cream sundae to top it off, strolled along the waterfront smoking cigars and turned in early for a deliciously quiet night. I don't mean to suggest that we were glad to leave Athos; we found it a thoroughly satisfying experience, particularly when we managed to leave the hordes of visitors behind. Dave later commented that some of the older monks were most impressive and certainly showed how one can grow old with peace and dignity.

EVIA

Summer Vacation

MY LOVE AFFAIR WITH THE GREEK ISLAND of Evia began when
Suzanne and I set out to explore it on a month long camping
trip. We had planned to leave Athens in the early morning before
the cocks crowed in our neighborhood nestled at the foot of the
Acropolis, Yes, as strange as it may seem Chanticleer and his breth-
ren announced the dawn to Athenians as they reluctantly rose to
start a new day. The feathered cry was clear in the morning air and
like clockwork, but for all the time I lived in Athens I never saw
one, nor knew anyone who had one. But I heard their refrain every
morning in the neighborhood of Koukaki.

Before the sun rose I had packed and loaded our gray, VW
Beetle lovingly christened "the Panzer" when I noticed that there
was an oil leak. The Panzer was indestructible and took us everywhere across fields and over the rough tracks that passed for roads
at that time. The one weakness that our indestructible Panzer suffered from, its Achilles Heel if you will, was the oil reservoir located
inches from the road. Over rough terrain, which was everywhere,
if one was not careful a glancing blow could crack the seal and a
slow leak would develop. Since this was to be our summer vacation camping all over the island, I didn't want to be driving around
leaking the Panzer's life's blood in the Homeric sod. As a result, I
unloaded the car which I had painstakingly packed with camping
gear and supplies for a month of travel. Now we were delayed until
9 a.m. when my VW service man, Sotiris, would be ready to fix the
leak.

I arrived hot and sweaty and told Mr. Sotiris what my problem was and furthermore what a struggle it had been to load and then unload the car. He directed me to his office festooned with tire ads featuring scantily clad ladies of pneumatic proportions. Once seated he lit a little camping stove and fixed me a 'metrio' the thick, sweetened Greek coffee which one could only drink halfway otherwise a mouth full of bitter grinds gagged the unwary. Once the ritual of making coffee was concluded he offered me a cigarette which I politely declined. Greeks were always horrified when I refused a cigarette. To them it wasn't so much a cigarette as the proffer of friendship. I could only refuse when the person knew me and my strange ways. In company a friend would say something to the effect, "This is my friend, Yourgo. He is an American." Everyone would then nod sagely as if that was enough to explain any eccentricities that I might exhibit. Through a cloud of smoke Sotiris studied me and commiserated. At the conclusion of my tale of woe, shaking his head, he said, "But my dear Yourgo, unloading the car was totally unnecessary. My lift could raise a tank off the ground. Didn't you take that into consideration?" Because he knew that I was a 'professor' at the University he was having a little fun with me, further adding to my deepening frustration.

Sotiris explained to his help what the 'professor' had done and we all enjoyed a good laugh at my expense. "Ahhh, the American!" In no time they replaced the gasket and sent me on my way. Sotiris refused payment because my story was a good one and he would take it home and regale his friends (parea) with the antics of the American Professor. A professor, an American, who does not know the power of a hydraulic lift! "'Hydraulic' it is a Greek word!"

Back at the house I am seething, because I have to repack the car and because as a result of this delay, the traffic through the city will be horrendous not to mention the madness we will face on the National Road. The last item to be loaded into the Panzer was

Sinafoula, our cat, a beautiful, normally mild-tempered Siamese. Her one failing was that she did not travel well. She hated the car. We had spoken to the vet about this problem and he recommended that we buy a cheap traveling case and prior to putting her in the case give her a quarter of a tablet of Dramamine. Seeing no result after administering a quarter of a tablet, I gave her another quarter and placed her into the traveling case and placed it in the car. Within seconds she had slashed her way out of "the cheap traveling case". It was made of cardboard. I administered a half a tablet, with no visible effect. She was clearly agitated and howling something fierce. I administered another half with the result that she lost all control over her hind legs! I had paralyzed our beautiful cat!

I called the vet, Dr. Demitri, and he was apoplectic. "No more Dramamine! I told you a quarter of a tablet. She will be OK. No more or you will truly kill her." As I hung up I heard him say to his assistant, " The American professor, he gave the cat almost two Dramamine!"

With Sinafoula yowling in my ear, we set off for our camping vacation. An acquaintance had told us about a "magical" spot that he and his wife had found on the island of Evia, about a four hour drive from Athens. Evia is located northeast of Athens and is the second largest island of all the islands surrounding mainland Greece. It is conveniently attached to the mainland by a bridge and as a result one did not have to worry about boat schedules. He described the place as a Mediterranean paradise 'paradisos', with fragrant pines stretching down to a sandy uninhabited beach, crystal clear water and wild thyme and oregano bushes scenting the air. So isolated and pristine that the whole family threw off their clothes and frolicked naked in the water. They had camped there for a week and would have stayed longer but they had found this idyllic spot at the end of their vacation and had run out of time and were obliged to return to Athens.

This then was our destination. The Greek road system at this time left much to be desired. Once you left the National Road many of the roads to outlying villages and towns were dirt tracks suitable only for donkeys. For these conditions the Panzer was admirably suited. But Fate further intervened when halfway to our destination a tire blew. I jacked up the overloaded car with the yoweling Sinafoula and found that the spare was missing. I had unloaded it when I was packing the car and forgot to replace it! On the hottest day of the year I removed the tire, wrestled the inner tube out and patched it. Now I needed to find a pump. But we were in the middle of nowhere and had passed a gas station hours ago on the National Road. In the distance I spied a farmhouse and hoping against hope that they might have an air pump set off, leaving my wife and the unhappy Sinafoula. I took the tire along with me in the event that the farmer would be reluctant to see a foreigner walk off with his pump. After a long, hot walk in the afternoon sun I arrived at the farmhouse where the farmer and his family were resting under a grape arbor. I could see that they were watching me as I approached their yard.

The farmer rose and said, "Good day, Sir. Are you looking for a car?" Ahh, I thought to myself, the gentleman has a sense of humor. "No, Sir, I am in need of a pump." And here my Greek failed me and I had to pantomime what I thought would convey the idea of a pump, much to the delight of everyone reclining in the shade. Now here I must digress for a moment. 'Sir' or 'Mr.' is a sign of respect that would be used with strangers or even friends. Especially in the country, villagers would address me very often as "Mr. or Sir" George. To show equal status I would address them as "Mr. or Sir Dimitri". This title was accorded me because they believed my status as a foreigner and as a 'professor' warranted this form of respect.

Eventually, a pump was found and after I was offered a glass of water and a teaspoonful, 'koutaliou', of a sweet jam, I started to pump up the tire. Normally I would politely decline the spoonful of sweets because it was enough to send the healthiest individual into a diabetic coma; however, I accepted it believing that I needed the jolt to get me back to the car. Of course I could not get away easily without, under not so subtle questioning, revealing my life story. Where I came from, where I was going and how I got myself in this mess was all grist for the mill. "The American, he left his spare tire at home!" More water and this time, shots of raki, the Greek equivalent of 'White Lightening', saw me off, marching unsteadily down the road attempting to catch a tire that seemed to be moving under its own will.

Back at the car Suzanne was hot and angry and when I tried to explain that I was only delayed because I had to accept the hospitality of the farmer and his family she quickly assessed the situation and said disgustedly, "You're drunk!" which was a fair analysis of my state. I reeked of raki and had a hard time focusing. Despite being under the influence, I placed the tire back on the car and as I lowered it to the ground the patch burst under the pressure. The situation was hopeless. We were stuck with no where to go. The closest town was thirty miles away. We would have to hitchhike, find a tire store and then hitchhike back probably in the dead of night. Foaming at the mouth I cursed the gods who had gotten us into this mess. I decided then and there that when we got a new tire we would go back to Athens and start out anew. The expedition was doomed.

Suzanne tried to placate me by suggesting we at least eat something before setting out. She had packed a chicken for our lunch. She unpacked it and the smell of rancid chicken even stopped Sinafoula from crying. Mind you she only paused before continuing her meows which were fortunately for my sanity getting weaker. The chicken had clearly not survived the heat.

Steeped in despair, at that moment a VW Bug roared passed, stopped and backed up. The driver got out and in fluent English asked us if he could help. I explained that the tire wasn't reparable and we would appreciate a ride to Halkida, the next town down the line. We explained our predicament and under close examination that is normal for Greeks meeting foreigners, he learned who we were, where we were from, my work, but the salary issue I was able to skirt. Greeks were always curious about how much money I earned. To ask it openly by my standard was something that was very personal and not just done. It was just one of those cultural differences that I had learned to uneasily live with. Once the preliminaries were over, he rubbed his chin very thoughtfully and a touch dramatically. He announced that we would take his spare and continue with our vacation! He would not have it any other way. He explained that he lived in Evia's main city of Halkida and had a VW dealership, the only one in town. When we returned from our vacation we could drop the tire off at his office. Everyone in town knew "VW Yiannis". With great pride he explained that good tires were a necessity to drive safely on Greek roads. His tires were brand new and he had no fear of a flat on his way back home. It was a magnanimous and slightly reckless gesture, but the longer I worked and lived with the Greeks I understood that this was a part of their nature. They would take food out of the mouths of their children to feed a 'xenos', a stranger. They were masters of the grand gesture even at a cost to them.

Our new friend helped me put his spare on my car. He gave us his phone number and with a wave drove off. Leaking oil pan, yow-eling cat, rancid chicken, and flat tire were enough for me to once again announce that we were going home. I had had it. Suzanne pointed out that we were not far from our destination, an isolated beach, pines down to the ocean, our own 'paradisos'. Grudgingly I agreed to continue our odyssey murmuring that 'paradisos' would probably turn out to be a boy scout camp or the new dump site for the village. Eventually we reached the village and turned down a rock strewn road that a donkey would have had a difficult time navigating. With visions of the oil pan being knocked through the roof we approached 'paradisos' at a snail's pace. Hot, tired and mentally strained to the breaking point we turned in to what was an active vacation camp for the employees of the Electric Company. There were hundreds of kids, and adults frolicking in the waters of our 'paradisos'.

This was it, the ultimate Greek experience, tragedy. Why shouldn't it happen to me? Look what happened to poor Oedipus on his way to Thebes and weren't the great writers, Euripides, Sophocles, Aeschylus tragedians all? Well, I wasn't going to blind myself on the road back from Shang-ri-la. But I was sure as hell getting out of Limni or whatever our Shang-ri-la was called. Suzanne suggested that we spend the rest of the day and night in a very small and very run down hotel in the village. Eyes bulging, veins popping I told her that I wanted to go home, I wanted a shower, I wanted something to eat and I wanted my own bed. I did not want to answer a million questions about who I was, where I came from and above all I didn't want to be quizzed on how much money I made. That was said all in one hysterical breath. On the way out of the village, Suzanne frantically consulted maps and guidebooks. She pointed out that at the next village, Aghia Anna, there was a ferry boat that would take us to the island of Skiathos. In this way we would escape from Evia which now held all the charm of Devil's Island. At this point my dear wife was weeping from heat exhaustion and my insane antics and pronouncements, and lest we forget Sinafoula's cries which were having the effect of the beating of the Tell Tale Heart. Madness lay just around the corner. The fates intervened at this point and I turned the wheel toward Aghia Anna, St. Anna's village. We took another boulder strewn road and headed uphill this time. "There won't be any ferry," I snarled, "And the village will have been decimated by the plague, mark my words" I muttered grimly.

View of Angali, Evia

We inched our way along until we reached the rise and spread below us was a two mile stretch of pristine beach with pine trees offering shade up to the water. On our way down we drove through groves of olive trees that flashed silver in the fading light. It was magic. We had found a little corner of paradise. We drove towards the heavily forested area that was south of the little village called 'Angali' which meant "embrace". We found an ideal spot to pitch our tent, and that was the end of our good fortune. After multiple attempts I could not get the paraffin lamp lit, so I had to use the car headlights to see what I was doing. The tent was quite spacious and it had to be erected in stages. In the last stage it would pop up to its full height which it did and was immediately smacked down by overhanging branches. I had to disassemble the whole tent and move it back and start all over again so that it could be properly raised without interfering branches. This task completed Suzanne suggested that we walk into town and have dinner. I barked and snarled no that I was not moving from the tent. I was tired, hungry, frustrated, aggravated and not fit for human company. If she wanted to walk into the village that was fine with me but this day of ill-omened events was not over and if she was attacked by wolves or the furies it was on her head and with that speech completed I collapsed on the camp bed and passed out.

The next morning we awakened to bird song and the sound of the waves of the blue Aegean crashing against the shore. The smell of fresh thyme and oregano filled the air because we had set up our tent in the midst of a field of it. The nightmare of the day before was over and we felt as if we had truly come into Elysian fields. We looked at each other and said, "Breakfast". We got into the car with the intention of driving into the village but the fates had one more trick to play. After using the lights to erect the tent, the battery was dead and we weren't going anywhere. With dread I wondered if the village would have a garage and the facility to charge the battery? Taking charge, I explained to Suzanne that the only thing we could do was to take the battery into the village and hope that there was a gas station there with the means to charge the battery. The town was about a mile away. I put the battery in a couple of plastic bags and off we walked to Angali. My arms felt as if I had spent an hour on the rack but we finally arrived at a seaside taverna and ordered breakfast. We feasted on fried eggs, honey and yoghurt, Nescafe coffee and fresh crusty bread straight from the oven. The owner of the taverna was named 'Yourgo', George, and since my name was George we bonded immediately. But that did not alter the ritual of who, what, where and why. After the preliminary interrogation I explained that our car had a dead battery and inquired if there was any place in the village that we could get it charged. I was informed that, unfortunately, the only garage that could charge batteries was miles away back in Halkida. He asked where the car was and I explained that it was a mile away in the forest, but I had the battery with me. He was amazed and not a little amused that I had lugged the battery more than a mile. He called over his son-in-law, Costa, and a few of the locals and explained what the American professor was up to. After much speculation a group decision was made.

Costa told me to leave Suzanne at the taverna with his mother-in-law and his wife and we, the men, would go back to the car. Back at the car, we placed the battery back where it belonged and an amused crowd pushed me until I got the car started and recharged the battery by driving everyone back to the taverna. That was our introduction to a place that we would call home for many years to come.

We passed lazy days on the beach. We saw no one because the locals all swam in the waters off the small town of Angali. Where we were located was considered forest and people preferred to swim where there was company. We cooked at the campsite and infrequently went down to Yourgo's taverna for dinner. There was a local farm down the road from our campsite and we bought tomatoes, peppers, eggplants and onions for a few drachmas and cooked up a big pot of ratatouille. The tomatoes smelled like a tomato and tasted rich, and it could be eaten as a meal in itself. The farmers used no fertilizers the soil was so rich. The farmer, Mr. Yiannis, Mr. John, was happy to sell us two tomatoes or an onion if that was all that we wanted. Or he would throw everything in our bag and charge us a few drachmas. Eggs were brought to us from the nest still warm and there was fresh goat's milk which we boiled and drank for breakfast. I felt like the early pioneers, with a little help from my new friends, living off the land, completely self sufficient. Clear skies, blue water, the scent of fresh pines, mountains at our back and miles of open beach, these were the simple pleasures that we enjoyed.

But for the unwary there were dangers in paradise. One day I was spear fishing off the beach while Suzanne was reading a book. I had just gone into the water for a look around and hadn't brought a net with me and since I was just spearing small fish I tucked them into my bathing suit. I shot a medium sized fish and went to take it off the spear. I didn't see that it had a sharp spine at the back of its head and as I grabbed it the spine jabbed me between my thumb and forefinger. Immediately I felt pain. It felt like an electric shock and the pain started to move up my arm. Suddenly I remembered a story a friend of mine told me about a fish that had the sting of a scorpion and if a fisherman was stung clearing his nets, having no first aid kit aboard, he would urinate on his hand to prevent the hand from being paralyzed which could happen if they were stung often enough. Clutching the fish I ran out of the water, threw the fish down, lowered my bathing suit, with fish flopping out all over the place, and I started urinating on my hand. Suzanne was wild eyed. Had I gone mad? I explained what had happened but even urinating on the hand didn't seem to help. The pain was pulsing up my arm. Would it reach my heart? Miles from any hospital, what could I do? Pulling up my suit I hurriedly told Suzanne that I was heading for the taverna to see it Yourgo could help me or direct me to the local doctor.

Driving like a madman I arrived at the taverna with fish in hand. Yourgo took one look at the fish and said, "Pain, you are in pain? " "Yes, I am in pain." I answered. But I felt I couldn't show how much because I didn't want the locals to think I was a sissy. I was the representative of the United States of America, so I had to put a good face on it. Yourgo called over the locals who echoed his sentiments. "Pain, the man is in pain!" Through gritted teeth I asked, "But what do I do? Where do I go. Is there a doctor up in Aghia Anna."? They explained that the doctor was attending a wedding in Athens. One man volunteered to go home and get some medicine that the doctor had given him. I was leery of that because he couldn't explain what the medicine was for. Yee gods was I going to die, fish in hand, on the taverna floor?. At that point as the men debated the best course of action, Mrs. Eleni, Yourgo's wife, grabbed me by the arm and took me behind the counter where they did all the cooking. She poured vinegar into a pot and heated it up. She removed the pot from the heat and directed me to put my hand in the vinegar and bear it as hot as possible. Miraculously the pain started to subside and I began to feel certain that my heart was no longer in danger and, as the Greeks say, I would not leave my bones in Angali.

We sat down and had ouzos all around and I had to tell the whole story of how I was fishing and putting the fish in my bathing suit when I speared the Scorpion fish. With a bold wink Yourgo said something to the other men that I didn't catch and everyone broke into hysterical laughter. I asked him to repeat what he said. He told me that if I had stuck the scorpion fish in my bathing suit, Mrs. Eleni would have needed a much bigger pot to boil the vinegar in. "Ahhh, the American, he almost put the scorpion fish in his bathing suit!"

A week later we were driving to Yourgo's taverna to fill up our five gallon water jugs when I noticed a young girl on a bicycle. I slowed down so that I could safely pass her and I saw that she was one of my EFL students from school. We saw each other simultaneously and stopped. I asked her what she was doing there and she replied in a stock phrase form our English book, "Sir, I live in a little house not far from here." Katerina was a motivated student. She loved English and quite honestly would have learned the language even without a teacher. I had met her mother on Parents' Night and she had declared me a genius for teaching her daughter English. Katerina pointed out her house. It was a two story stone house in the center of the village with an extensive garden all around it. She invited us back to her house after we had finished our errands.

We were welcomed like long lost relatives. We sat in the garden and were offered cold well water, the infamous jam on a spoon which I managed to switch for an ouzo. The hospitality that was extended was overwhelming. When the mother, Tassia, heard that we were camping, living in a tent, in the forest, she crossed herself. This couldn't be. How could her daughter's teacher be living in a tent like a gypsy? Impossible, rumbled Loukas, the father. Loukas was a lawyer and had a tremendous amount of gravitas. When he spoke everyone listened. He was the head of the family, but like in all Greek families, the mother took care of the everyday affairs and the father concerned himself with important things like politics and football scores. We were instructed to pack up immediately and bring our belongings to the house. Grandma would move in with Katerina and we would have Grandma's room! We were startled by the offer. The reason we camped was because we loved the opportunity to be so close to nature and yet be entirely on our own. To the Greek way of thinking this was anathema. Privacy had negative connotations. Without friends, parea, how could one live alone? The Greek is a very social animal and without the stimulation of friends and family they feel cut off. How did we eat, where did we go to the toilet and what did we do all day?

To allay their concerns we invited them to dinner the following night. The menu consisted of barbecued chicken, a big Greek salad, consisting of tomatoes, cucumbers, onions, feta cheese and a dressing of plain olive oil. But the biggest hit was the potatoes that we wrapped in foil and baked in the coals of our fire. The campsite drew their admiration. We were in a pine grove with a view of the beach and the Aegean. Loukas waxed lyrical and recounted tales from his youth when as a young boy he would camp with his village friends. But still they where uneasy that we were so isolated. I explained that we were able to read, study and prepare lesson plans so that I could teach Katerina and her friends the following year. The pressure for us to move in with the family eased when we agreed to have lunch or dinner with them from time to time, so that they would know wild animals had not eaten us. And so at least two or three times a week we would dine at their home. The meals were fabulous. Tassia could have cooked rocks and we would have gladly eaten them. Many of the dishes were cooked in a form of lard called Vitam, which we knew wasn't necessarily good for you.

However her stuffed tomatoes, pasta, and lamb dishes were gastronomic treats. Everything was always washed down with copious amounts of wine that had been made from their own grapes. We erroneously believed that the wine offset the effects of the artery clogging Vitam.

THE HOUSE

OUR INTENTION HAD BEEN TO CAMP on Evia and then visit other places, but we were so taken with Evia that we spent our two months vacation in our little piece of paradise. Tassia and Suzanne began to conspire about the possibility of buying a piece of land. A half an acre at that time was between three and five thousand dollars, not an insignificant sum in 1967 on the salary of a teacher. But money wasn't the main problem. Finding a seller was the big problem. Once a seller was found they would become very cagey. The going price was between three and five thousand dollars, but if a foreigner was involved should the price go higher? So, a seller would be found, negotiations begun and then the seller would say something to the effect that he had to check back with his wife and that was usually the last time that we would hear from him.

However, we did have some strong cards to play. Tassia was from the village and knew everyone in and around the village and Loucas was a lawyer so that all negotiations would be handled legally and properly. This was very important to me because as a foreigner I didn't want to be put in a position of having the land taken away from us by the government or anyone else due to a technicality. Just as things were looking hopeless, Tassia arrived at the campsite one day and said that she had found a motivated seller. She showed us the land that was definitely for sale. It was a half an acre, a corner property, one block from the beach and a couple of blocks from our campsite. It was ideal, but we had to meet the owner and negotiate the price which could be anywhere, hopefully, between three and five thousand dollars. The meeting was to take place the following day at Loucas and Tassia's house. I was keyed up. How do I bargain? I had never bargained for anything this big in my life. Should I open with the standard line that the property is not what I am looking for? But that could lose me the sale and we desperately wanted the land. We arrived at the house at the appointed hour and Tassia rushed out and as we were walking into the house she said that the deal was done. She had agreed to a price of five thousand dollars and now all we had to do was meet the couple, drink some ouzo and shake hands. Five thousand was at the top end of the scale, but what the heck. We wanted that land so badly we would have paid much more. We were introduced to the elderly couple and exchanged pleasantries. At one point I leaned over to Suzanne and in sotto voce, said that he looked like a right old pirate and she nodded her assent. As the ouzo was being poured the 'old pirate' in Greek asked Tessia if by any chance the young couple were Americans? We answered for ourselves that yes, indeed, we were Americans. In flawless English he informed us that for many years he had owned a seafood snack bar in Times Square. He was extremely pleasant and we chatted about New York and Times Square. If he had heard the 'old pirate' remark he was gracious in not referring to it. With the sun sinking into the wine dark Aegean Sea the deal was done. We owned the land but our adventure was only beginning.

Camping on our Land

The following summer we camped on "our land". We had a well dug by one of the local farmers. He started digging at 8 a.m. and by noon we were drinking crystal clear water from our well. The land had pine trees and lots of scrub oak. We camped under the pines and visitors always asked us when we were going to clear the land. We always responded that we wanted to leave the land in its natural state and didn't intend to clear it. We should have heeded these inquiries, but we were so intent on being in tune with nature that we never thought to ask why we needed to clear the land. It appeared to us that it was the custom to clear the land, but we were not going to follow custom in this matter.

Our only neighbors for miles were an Austrian couple, Philip and Eda and a large Greek family, the Tangas. Philip was a Greek who had gone to Germany as a guest worker but when the Second World War broke out he became a slave laborer for the Nazis. He survived the war and he met Eda in Vienna and stayed and went into business in Austria. Every summer they came back to Greece for two months. Many nights we went to their house and drank wine and listened to him the play the guitar. One night in his fractured English he explained that he knew some hillbilly songs. He asked me if I knew "Vandering". I said that I had never heard of it and suggested that he play it. It turned out to be "Wondering", "wondering, wondering who's kissing you, etc." At the beginning of the summer he would purchase about a dozen crates of wine and by the end of the summer only the empty crates remained along with many happy memories.

One evening we were sitting by our well, drinking ouzo and munching on canned sardines when Philip came by with a young man who clearly was in the building trade since his boots were covered in cement and his grip was firm and rough from handling cement blocks. Philip informed us that George had built his house and if anyone was going to build our house, George was our man. We invited them to sit down and join us for an ouzo. We explained that we didn't have the money to build a house since we had only purchased the land the previous year, but out of curiosity we asked what it would cost to build a house like the one he had built for Philip. George told us that it would cost about three and a half thousand dollars. It was not an unreasonable sum. We took out a paper bag and started drawing a floor plan. When we were through with our sketch which was larger than Philip's house George said that we were looking at a cost of five thousand dollars "with the key" which meant everything included.

We explained to George that it was a reasonable offer but one beyond our means, but we would certainly keep it in mind. Then he made us an offer that left us speechless. He informed us if we could raise a thousand dollars for the building supplies, he would build the house and we could pay him whenever we had the rest of the money. Suzanne and I looked at each other and then wondered aloud if we had missed something in the translation? But no, he insisted that we had a deal. All we had to do was give him the equivalent of a thousand dollars and he would start to build in September and we would be able to move into our house in June. All he needed from us were more formal blueprints and once he had them he would begin work. He assured me that once he had the plans he would submit them to the authorities and obtain the building permit. Knowing that things were not always done legally in the village, I emphasized the fact that I had to have a permit because after all I was a foreigner and I couldn't afford to be on the wrong side of the law. In Greece very specific laws could be passed that would stipulate, for example, an American, of Italian decent from New York City did not have the right to build a house on the island of Evia. George and Philip assured me that everything would be legal.

At the end of the summer when I went back to work a colleague who was a civil engineer drew up the plans, but he asked me if I was out of my mind. How could I hand over a thousand dollars to someone without a legal contract? I explained that George was satisfied with a handshake and that was good enough for me. I was told in no uncertain terms that I was a fool. I had to have a contract with terms regarding the time table for building and the payment of the thousand dollars, etc. He drew up the contract for us along with the plans. In September we met with George at his house and his wife, Eleni. We ate grilled pork chops grilled in the fireplace and we drank their homemade, ruby red wine. I showed George the plans and the contract. He appeared slightly offended by the contract but signed it. He looked me in the eye and told me that the paper meant nothing. What was in our hearts was more important than any piece of paper.

We got into details. The fireplace wall was to have a brick finish. George was astounded by this. He explained that brick and cement block had to be covered with plaster otherwise the room would look unfinished. It would look like an old house. We explained that was what we wanted. We wanted the house to look like an old house. What really caused him to pause and regard us as completely mad was that we wanted beams in the ceiling. Why would anyone build a new house and want to make it look old? It just didn't make any sense to him. Finally I reminded him that we were foreigners, Americans, and he knew that we were all a bit mad. He smiled, nodded and excused himself. Five minutes later we heard a thumping on the stairs outside. In a heavy downpour, over his shoulder he hauled up a gnarled log. He asked us if this was what we wanted in our ceiling and we told him that it was perfect. We now had the two main features of the living room, our fireplace set in an unfinished brick wall and rafters to complete our country home.

The work moved along quickly despite all the gloomy warnings that friends kept assailing us with. "He will take your money and leave you high and dry. The work will never be completed on time. He will come back and ask for more money." Our Greek friends were the most disbelieving and negative. "Who ever heard of such an offer, pay when you get the money! Impossible" Despite all the nay saying, each week we saw progress, first the foundation, then the columns, then the roof and finally the walls and windows. One weekend we arrived to find the fireplace and the brick wall completed. We hailed George as a master builder and a genius. Now all of this of course was conducted in fractured Greek because we had not by any stretch of the imagination become proficient in Greek. At some point George remarked that it would be even more beautiful once it was painted. We weren't sure what he was referring to; of course we were going to paint but not the brick wall.

The House

The following week we drove to the house and at quite a distance I could see through the windows a bright fire engine red wall. Our natural brick wall had been painted fire engine red and very carefully the mortar between the bricks had been painted a gunmetal gray. Suzanne was apoplectic. I attempted to calm her down.

I explained that George was building to specifications that he had never dealt with and clearly he had not painted the wall out of spite. The time to paint it must have set him back at least two days, to hand paint each brick and then to paint the mortar in between. When into him despite my best efforts to calm her down. I could see that George was initially puzzled and then hurt by her reaction. His guileless response "But I did it to make it more beautiful." That set her off again. Finally after she had exhausted herself, George looked at her and said, "Mrs. Suzanne why are you so filled with anger?" And quite simply George put his finger on an underlying character trait that bedeviled her and our relationship. It wasn't the last time that I learned truths about people, events and even history from supposedly uneducated villagers. They always showed me great respect because I was "educated", but, in truth, I learned much more from them. Over the years George did many projects for me and it was never with more than a handshake. He loved his work and was a joyous man who told me that the secret to his marriage was told to him by his father, "Never go to bed angry at your spouse!" You always knew where he was working because he loved to sing. My friend's voice was silenced one year when his tractor overturned. He was buried on the hill overlooking Angali where he had built so many beautiful homes.

Our friends Philip, George and Eleni

By June first the house was complete "With the key". And since we had come into a little money we were able to pay George five thousand dollars or a hundred and fifty thousand drachmas. We were the proud owners of land and a house on the island of Evia. But as so often happened disaster was never too far off.

FOREST FIRE

IT WAS A QUIET SUNDAY MORNING when billowing gray and white smoke signaled the start of a forest fire, behind the hills, kilometers away from our newly completed island home. We spotted the fire precisely at 11:00 a.m. in the morning. I remember the hour well because we were trying to figure out how long it would take the chicken to be ready for our lunch at 1:00 p.m. At one o'clock the chicken was ready but our thoughts were elsewhere up on the ridge line as it exploded sending sparks, smoke, and orange and yellow flames dancing down the hillside, moving with the inexorable force of molten lava. The air became filled with white ash and the bitter, acrid smell of smoke fed by pine trees bursting into sheets of flame. The agony of the dying trees was intensified as the tins of draining pine resin nailed to their sides exploded. The demonic force of the flames was fed by a hot wind coming off the hills blowing towards the sea. The only thing between this cataclysm of fire and the sea was my new house and the seven souls who had been invited for a weekend in the country, and one of them was only a year old Now before this fateful day neighbors had come by to congratulate me on the completion of my new house. They were curious why we chose a property so far from the village, out in the woods with no one else around us. We could have found a plot of land in the little town and sat on our porch and conversed with the neighbors surrounding us. We explained that we liked the serenity, but they could not accept the fact that we chose to be alone, in their minds isolated. There is no word for privacy in Greek. It is a word that has negative connotations. No Greek knowingly chooses isolation. The Greek is a social being to his very core. But we were foreigners and they accepted the fact that we were different and so be it. The other issue that they raised and which I quickly dismissed was in regard to the clearing of the land. I had purchased half an acre of land and set the house on a clear space right under a gigantic old pine tree that afforded us shade. The rest of the land was overrun with small to medium sized pine trees and scrub oak, 'pornaria', a favorite meal for goats. "You will clear the land?" my neighbors queried. "No," we responded, "We want to leave it natural." We had half an acre and clearing it seemed a daunting challenge. What did one do with all that land once it was cleaned off. The ground was sand. You couldn't grow anything. I was just a city boy and we did not measure acreage where I came from. The neighbors would greet our response with a certain amount of puzzlement, and they would shake their heads. They accepted the answer. After all we were foreigners, we were different. In my ignorance, nay arrogance I never asked them "Why"? " Is there a reason I should clear the land?" Would I have accepted their reason? Would they have known why, other than it was a tradition? When you bought land you cleared it put a fence around it and later you would build. To them it was quite simple.

I watched the 'pornaria' disintegrating into howling flames and I understood in an incandescent burst of clarity why it was necessary to clear the land. The pornaria was so green, but it burned like gasoline soaked newspapers. The fire raced along the ground and it flew overhead as pine cones exploded sending fiery sparks heavenward. It sounded like the crushing of enormous sheets of cellophane paper. For the moment we were all alone. Six adults and a baby. We told ourselves that we had a few advantages. We had access to water. There was a newly dug well on the property and a new gasoline engine to bring the water up to a tank on top of the flat concrete roof of our house. We could also pump it through a 20 foot, 2 inch hose.

Our neighbors came by to tell us that they were going off to the olive groves to fight the fire on the front line, so to speak. We joined them believing that we would be able to team up with other villagers and perhaps stop the fire before it reached our house. We arrived at the groves to find that there was no organized resistance. Each man or family had run off to their own section haphazardly addressing the flames. There was no equipment, no tools. Men and boys broke off branches and began attempting to flail the fire, more frequently than not fanning the flames to greater intensity. They were dressed in bathing suits or shorts and sandals which gave no protection from the sparks and flames. We didn't stay very long, realizing the futility of their efforts. As we turned towards home we came to the sobering conclusion that we would not escape the fire's path. Once home we asked Suzanne to drive the two cars onto the beach and to stay there with the other two women and the baby while we grimly prepared ourselves for the onslaught. At that point my neighbors returned expressing their frustration with the actions of their neighbors and the townspeople who refused to come down and help fight the fire in the olive groves. What could we say? My faithful neighbor and friend, Stamatis took me aside and told me not to worry. Everything would be all right. He said that he and his brother Apostoli were going for help up to the main village for help. The flames were coming closer. We shook hands and I wished him good luck. It felt like a moment out of *'Beau Geste'*.

I didn't expect to see him again because the flames did not appear to be on a course for his house and he had no real reason to return. I could not imagine what help he would find in the village, but he had always proved to be resourceful and maybe just maybe he would galvanize the other villagers into action. Anything was possible. Still hoping against hope that the strong wind pushing the avalanche of flame towards us would die down, we dressed ourselves and waited.

It was not long before the flames leaped the road in front of the house and fires started breaking out on the property all around us. The smoke choked you, the flames seemed to suck the breath out of your body. Some more neighbors came over and we thought that with the extra help we could form a bucket brigade and direct the maximum amount of water on a particular area while one of us manning the hose would hit another sector. We were all scared and not thinking correctly but for us, the foreigners, there was an added element, we were trying to do things in a foreign language. So the bucket brigade idea had to be pantomimed first. But it soon proved a shambles not through our linguistic inadequacies but because of a fundamental characteristic of the Greek. Each man wanted to run with the bucket. No matter how much I begged or cajoled whoever got his hands on the bucket ran off with it and usually in a different direction. My friend Bill found me weeping and laughing. But that all stopped immediately when I saw his face. He pointed out that the beautiful, enormous, ancient pine that I had built the house in the shade of was in danger of going up in flames. Bill yelled, "We have to get up on the roof and direct the hose on that tree or everything will go up in flames." We raced up the stairs to the roof and I hurriedly attached a length of hose to the inlet pipe on the water tank while he raced downstairs and cranked up the motor. I was standing in the shade of this enormous smoking tree with a pitiful little hose in my hands realizing that I would be just as effective if I tried to pee on it. At that moment Bill raced up and shouted that we had to get the hell out of there because when that tree went it would take us with it like a moth to a flame. He was wild eyed and I thought, "What the hell he's right". This is a guy who survived Vietnam and I knew him generally to be cool and laid back. What he was saying made sense and the tree looked ready to go. We dropped the hose and fled down the stairs. Bill ran off to tackle our hydra headed bucket brigade.

Just at that moment one of the farmers who had come to help ran up and said, "Mr. George, we have to get water onto that tree or it will destroy the house." Without a minute's hesitation I ran back up the stairs with him and we again started to wet down the tree. I laughed to myself as we wet down the tree. There was no logic to anything that we were doing. We were possessed by a frenzy of fear and confusion not unlike what historians refer to as the "fog of war."

From the roof I had a bird's eye view of the fire and the surrounding area. I glanced over at the road and saw a dust cloud rising as a pickup drove the length of the forest road with flames snatching at it. As it came closer I could hear the horn sounding its coming. It was Stamatis driving like a fury through all that chaos. Flames were burning on both sides of the road and I feared for his life. It was the most courageous and insane thing I had ever seen, driving into the heart of the flames. To what purpose? He was not in the vanguard of a relief column. There were no tools or men in the back of the truck. What the hell was he doing? As they came closer I saw what they had done and what they were attempting to accomplish Stamatis drove like a man possessed, Apostoli hung out the passenger's side with the Holy icon of St. Anna from the church. The icon was a large, ornate painting of St. Anna on a wooden board. St. Anna was the patron of the village which was named in her honor. They were attempting to stem the tide of flame and keep it from the properties on our side of the road. I expected them at any moment to burst into a fire ball: but they drove safely past. Minute later they came hurtling back to repeat their quixotic performance. This time the icon was safely tucked in the cab. But it was too late for miracles. We had saved the house but most of our trees and plants had been scorched.

By nightfall the offshore breeze had dropped and the force of the fire was spent. Our friends Chip and Aliki with their baby returned to Athens and Bill and I slept on the roof in shifts staying awake to be certain that the fire did not break out again. A fire company showed up along with some elements of the army but the firemen just drove along the road and sprayed water on the sides of the road. The soldiers filled up the cafes and sat around drinking coffee. It seemed no one wanted to go into the forest and get their uniforms or the vehicles dirty. This was before the days of real organization that used planes bearing water and chemicals. We spent the next day wetting everything down. The floor of the forest was hot for days. The trees had burned with such intensity that in many cases the roots were still burning underground. At midnight the following night I told Suzanne that I was going to sleep in bed and that if the fire restarted, I didn't really give a damn. Let it burn. I took off my pants and they were so stiff from water, ash and smoke that they literally stood up in the corner of the bedroom.

At three o'clock in the morning Suzanne shook me and said that there was someone outside calling my name. I staggered out to the porch and saw that it was my neighbor, Walter, a German from Munich. He told me that he had been keeping watch and he saw a fire in a section of the forest that had been spared, but he was unsure how to reach it. Would I go with him? I couldn't refuse. His house was in no danger but he was keeping watch for the rest of us. We drove along the forest road in his Volvo which I later found was filled with 5 gallon plastic jugs of water. He had spent the day driving into the forest putting out hotspots.

As we drove along he told me how upset he had been by the villagers' attitude.

"Tchorch, ven I saw the fire I vent up to the village and dey vere ringing der bells. Dat is good I tink because in Chermany ven you have such a catastrof all der men run to der villitch center. You are given orders and you go to fight der fire. It is der law. It is like you vas in der army. Only der sick and der old are excused. Vell wehn I reach der church dey stop ringing der bells and they start ringing der hands. And they say "Panagia (Holy Virgin) safe us." "I tink dis is not der Panagia's business." He shook his head sadly, "I got sick with dem and went to help my neighbor Yiannaki. We bounced along and went into the forest as far as we could and then we went in on foot. The forest was mysterious at that hour silent and black. The smell of burnt pine was strong. In the distance we could see a flame burning brightly in a wooded area that somehow survived the flames. It looked like a spectral campfire. It burned straight up and did not flicker. There was absolutely no wind at that hour and not a sound. We sat there transfixed by the flame. We were unable to reach it because of the dense underbrush. I fully expected to see a demon or a spirit start to dance around this solitary flame. In the end we decided that it was harmless and would burn itself out. We walked back to the car in silence each deep in his own thoughts.

GRANDMA SAYS GOOD-BYE

BEFORE THE FLAMES STRUCK THE PROPERTY we decided that Suzanne would drive our friend's VW van to the village. Earlier the cars had been driven down to the beach, but it was felt that the three women and the baby who were staying with us would be safer and more comfortable in the seaside village rather than in the direct path of the smoke and flames. The smoke and ash were making it hard for everyone to breathe. Suzanne had never driven a van before even though the gear shift was the same as the VW Bug that we drove. It was the size of the van that was off putting, but she managed it and brought everyone safely to our local Taverna run by George and Elleni. The scene at the Taverna was fraught with drama and hysteria. At one point someone came running up screaming, "Put the women and children into the sea before they are all burned alive." Cooler heads prevailed and the women and children were spared being forced to stand up to their necks in the Aegean for several hours.

After Stamatis and Apostoli finished their wild ride with the icon, they packed up their wives and children and left them off at the Taverna for safe keeping. It appeared that their house wasn't in danger so they went off to the olive groves to see if they could save some of their trees. Evangelia, Stamatis wife, approached Suzanne and informed her that in the excitement of rushing from the house they had forgotten her mother (Yiaya) who was bedridden and lying outside under the shade of an enormous pine tree. Suzanne was horrified. No one knew which way the flames would go. She decided that they had to go back through the gauntlet of fire and bring Yiaya out. Our house guest Aliki spoke Greek and asked one of the men to drive the van down to Stamati's house to rescue the grandmother but no one would go. They said that it was too dangerous and besides she was old and was going to die anyway. They viewed it all as very practical, after all, life was precious and she had lived her life. Even Stamatis and the family would talk about the grandmother in that sense. "Next year when Grandma dies." In a way this is what I found fascinating about the villagers. Their lives centered around planting and holidays and the natural rhythm of life, the seasons, birth, marriage, holidays and ultimately death. It was all to be reckoned with.

Suzanne was having none of it. In her limited Greek she berated them and called them cowards. It was a big mistake on her part. They ignored her. But two young boys from a neighboring village who spoke some English approached Suzanne and told her that they would be willing to go, but unfortunately they did not know how to drive. If Suzanne would drive, they would go with her, thereby inadvertently throwing her challenge back in her face. She did not hesitate even though the van was not hers. Aliki who owned the van gave her blessing sure that her husband Chip who was with me fighting the fire, would have given his blessing also. Suzanne, Aliki and the two boys went back up the road into the flames. Not at all comfortable with the van and being thrown around on the dirt road the two boys encouraged her to drive as fast as possible. The smoke and the flames were frightening. Once past our house things looked normal and they arrived at Stamatis' house safely. They found grandma under the pine tree. She had smelled the smoke and had seen the ash but was unaware of her predicament. She was surprised to see Suzanne and asked where everyone was and if they were safe. She was very light and the boys carried her gently to the van and made her comfortable.

For the rest of the summer and that winter grandma regaled everyone with the miracle of her escape from the forest fire and her gratitude to Suzanne who saved her from the flames. Suzanne and

I were very attached to Yiaya because though she was loved and well cared for by the family, they took her for granted. Her usefulness was finished. She couldn't weave, take care of the goats or help harvest the olives, make cheese, cultivate the garden or do any other of the tasks for which the women were responsible. She could just crack the walnuts for the walnut pies and she could tell stories. We would sit with her and talk to her and listen to a story, but the family would always call us to table and make us understand that we were wasting our time. They were not cruel. They loved her dearly but her usefulness was at an end. She died the following summer.

I believe she died at the end of July and the family invited us up to the village for the funeral which was to be held in the late afternoon at around five o'clock. I didn't want to go. I knew that there would be lamentations and weeping and the coffin would be opened one last time at the graveside. The mourners would then return to Stamatis' house and everyone would have bean soup and drink wine. Suzanne was annoyed with me and insisted that I go because it was our obligation being so close to the family. I told her to go and tell them that I was unwell. I just felt it was going to be a party and I did not want to be any part of it.

I had finished my chores for the day and had showered outside in the garden and had put on fresh shorts and a shirt. It was around 5:30 or 6:00 p.m. and it was dead calm as it usually is at that time of day. The wind drops and then the offshore breeze gently picks up later in the evening. The sun was still hot and the doors and windows were all open. My plan was to have my own memorial service. I was going to have an ouzo on the front porch and watch the sun go down over the hills. I felt that this would be a more fitting observance of Yiaya's passing. I poured myself an ouzo and set it on the dining room table and turned back to the bedroom to get my sunglasses when the front door slammed with an almighty, crack. At the same time the glass of ouzo fell off the table and shattered into hundreds of pieces. No other door or window slammed everything was calm, dead calm and silent. The hairs on the back of my neck rose. Instinctively I knew that Yiaya had come to say good-bye to the beach and me. I have never believed in ghosts and do not to this day. I don't even believe in ESP or parapsychology but I know for a fact on that day in July, Yiaya came to say good-bye.

Stamatis and Evangelis

Months later I was speaking to Evangelia and Eleni, Apostoli's wife, and I told them what had happened. I was curious to see their reaction but they said nothing and just exchanged a glance between themselves. There was something in that glance which made me understand that I had been very privileged on the day of Yiaya's funeral.

MR. LOUKAS

THOUGH GEORGE HAD PROMISED to take care of the building permit and any other legal obligations, I learned to my horror that my house was built 'illegally". I learned this one day when the local policeman came by the house requesting to see the permit. I explained that George had taken care of that and I would get back to him. I went to George's house and told him about the visit and asked for the permit. He smiled and informed me that 'no one' built with a permit because it was totally illegal to build where we were anyway. Our area was designated as forest and by law no one could build in an area with that designation. George said that he would take care of the police and I never heard from them again. I learned later that most of the houses built in and around the village were illegal for different reasons, but no one seemed particularly concerned.

However, it did mean that we would not be able to obtain any utilities, water, electricity, phone, sewerage, etc. that would eventually come into the area.

Loukas had handled all the papers for the sale of the land and had become my lawyer forever. He refused to accept any money because for them it was a point of honor. Not only was I Katerina's teacher, but I was a friend. On a number of occasions I realized how fortunate I was in having Loukas as counsel. Generally speaking you needed a lawyer when you were dealing with the bureaucracy of that time. The normal run-around that one got from the civil service was Kafkaesque. It would take me several days to gear myself up before going to a government office. It was the most uncivil service that I had ever dealt with. They would usually start off by sending you from room to room where clerks snarled at you and by their ferocious demeanor just dared you to inconvenience them. You inevitably ended up back in the office that you had first started out from. I usually adopted my most humble stance and was duly deferential as deferential as one might be to a foreign potentate who held the power of life or death over you. It worked. My tactic was to try and make them feel sorry for me and show them that I really was not a threat in any way. Sort of the way you would behave around if you were in a cage with a four hundred-pound orangutan. There was one type of clerk that you had to beware of and that was the man who had a long nail on his pinky. This indicated that he did not do manual labor. It was indicative of someone who was very sensitive about his status. You had to be very careful in addressing him because he would be quick to show offense and he could make your life a misery.

Years later during an election period the government passed a law that allowed all illegal buildings to be legalized so that you could then apply for utilities and be legal in the eyes of the law. This was the opportunity to get the building permit that George had not been able to get for me. For this task I had to go to the capital of the island, Halkida, and apply for the permit, pay for tax stamps and present all manner of documents. I knew that if I tried to do this by myself it would take months and possibly my best efforts would come to naught. I called Loukas and asked for his help. We arranged a date to drive from Athens to Halkida a trip of about one and a half hours. Loukas was of the old school. He was always formally dressed, a man of large girth and basso profoundo voice which came from years of smoking Pall Malls. He was hard of hearing and compensated for it by bellowing at all and sundry. He was too vain to wear a hearing aid. After all it was not his problem. The rest of the world just had to speak louder. As I have said in my forays with the bureaucracy I always maintained a low profile and tried to ingratiate myself with the petty mandarins. But I knew that placing myself in the hands of Loukas was going to be another matter.

Almost immediately he showed me his style. People were on line outside of the building and I suspect on the same errand as we. When I went to take my place in the line Loukas grabbed by the arm and growled, "Follow me." We went into the first office and he literally burst into the room without knocking. We found the three standard clerks and six cups of coffee and cigarette befogged atmosphere. "Who's in charge here?" he rumbled. The room was electrified. The clerks snapped to attention. Even those people who were being served stepped back from the counter indicating recognition that they were in the presence of an important personage. He stated his business so that the locals in the kafenion across the street were aware of what we were up to. One of the clerks rose to challenge the manner in which he had entered the room and addressed them. Loukas swatted him like a fly "Where is the Director!" It wasn't a question. It was a statement with the implication that he was not used to dealing with anyone of a lower order. Suddenly one of the women who seemed to be the only one working in the office said "Cousin Loukas, how are you. How is Tassia and Katerina?" He fixed her with a steely glance and smiled in recognition thus breaking the tension "Panayiota, is that you, koritsi mou (my girl? She was fifty if she was a day.) He said, "Listen this man is an American and the director of a large school in Athens and he doesn't have time to waste. We must get him a permit." I cringed. The socialists were in power and Andreas Papandreou was now Prime Minister, ex US citizen, ex Professor of Economics at Berkeley and regularly continued bashing the U.S. holding it responsible for whatever ills at the moment beset the country. We were not as popular as we had been when I first arrived in Greece. Most of these people in the civil service owed their jobs to the new government and therefore were in sympathy with its policies. My citizenship was the last thing that I wanted to publicize in this office. But Loukas had the family connection and in

Greece that was heavy "meson" (roughly translated 'the inside track' or 'connection'). Obstacles and details were dispensed with, with the speed of summer lightening. A tame civil engineer was found to go out and survey the property, stamps were paid for and pourboires (tips) dispensed at Loukas' discretion. Panayiota sent us on our way with a dozen fresh eggs from her henhouse. All in all it was a very satisfying bit of business. The fines and stamps were not excessive. I ended up paying about as much as I would have paid if I could have originally applied for a building permit.

Years later when Suzanne and I had divorced I bought her share of the house. The problem that arose from this transaction was that we had to pay taxes on the property just as in any other sale. I could not avoid the taxman even if she had wanted to give me her share. This was the first time in twenty years that the property was to be evaluated. Loukas had retired by then but he said that he would come to the tax office in Limni with me to see what he could do. I had to endure the ride while Loukas chain smoked Pall Malls. I did not know it at the time nor did the family, but Loukas was eighty five years old. Fifteen years older than his wife thought he was! His hearing was worse but his mind was sharp. Driving up from Athens we agreed that we would tell the taxman that I had bought out my ex-wife for ten thousand dollars. In reality I had paid her twenty-five but our object was to low ball everything to keep the tax to a minimum. Loukas warned me that our mission was a difficult one. He was afraid the tax man would be a socialist or god forbid even a communist. "We will see." he rumbled ominously.

When we arrived he dealt with the menials as he had done before in Halkida. We were informed that the "efforos" the chief taxman was out and no one knew when he was coming back. As a matter of fact we might have to go back to Athens and make an appointment for another day. This was not unusual and I had foreseen that something like this could happen. Loukas said that we would wait and as it happened the efforos returned. Loukas' demeanor changed. He spoke as one potentate to the other. The efforos was a young man but obviously comfortable with his powers. The key would be to establish some rapport, find a common acquaintance, relative, friend almost anything to establish some connection. Finding out his political preference would be very tricky. Loukas was conservative to his fingertips and he despised communists and believed that socialists were wolves in sheep's clothing. He and his generation remembered the terrible civil war.

As they sat and sparred I suddenly realized that I had forgotten what sum we had agreed upon as the sale price. I was panic stricken and I tried to whisper to Loukas at one point when the efforos was on the phone. Loukas did not respond to whispers. You had to stand an inch from his ear and bellow. I kept my fingers crossed that I would not be called upon to play any role in the negotiations. The initial discussions were not fruitful. I could see that Loukas could not find any common ground and the efforos, clearly very experienced, was not volunteering any information. When Loukas told him the sum of money that was involved the efforos laughed. In a way it was a game. He expected us to lie and we would bargain, if we were lucky, for the final price. He called for the ledger that listed properties in our area and said that the last land had been taxed at the rate of 600,000 drachmas ($20,000.). I had $5,000 with me. Things were not looking too good. Loukas rumbled his outrage and the efforos nodded sympathetically. He said that he would have to see the land, and it turned out that he was free and willing to go that very minute. At least that was one break. We wouldn't have to go back to Athens and return another day.

It was an hour's drive and we drove in my car. In the course of the drive, Loukas used every trick to find out where the efforos was from. He was amazing, not subtle but persistent. It turned out that the efforos was from Evia. Loukas knew the town "If you are from Xidi, then you must have had Pantelides as your teacher?" "Yes" replied the efforos noncommittally. And slowly from there

Loukas continued probing. He named people that he knew in the town. He found out the efforos' university, his army career, but we were still unsure of his politics. I was getting the impression that we were in the presence of a decent young man who was tasked with an important responsibility and was trying to do his job well under great difficulties. But was he for us or against us? Did we have any room to maneuver? Would we be treated fairly? Six hundred thousand drachmas was almost twenty thousand dollars.

We arrived at the house and the efforos noted that there was a substantial garage and tool house on the property that we had not mentioned. Well, we didn't think it mattered we muttered weakly. He indicated that his inspection was finished and we could go back to Limni. He said ominously, " I have seen everything I have needed to see." "Mr. Efforos, a cup of coffee would be in order." Loukas proffered. "We could have a cup of coffee at Kyritsi's place." "I prefer Gavril's," said the Efforos and my heart leapt. Gavril had been a gendarme back in the fifties. The efforos had to be a conservative! Every little bit helped. When we walked into Gavril's taverna the owner, bless his heart, treated me like a long lost son even though I tended to frequent Kyritsis' place. The efforos was warmly welcomed. The efforos seemed to have some family connection with Gavril.

Loukas was jubilant. Things were looking up. On the ride back the efforos mellowed and he shared some remembrances with Loukas. We were not out of the woods yet, but things were definitely looking up. When we got back to his office, the efforos again called for the ledgers and they were brought in by a balding, stoop shouldered gentleman in his fifties. He stopped in his tracks with the books in his arms and said, "Mr. Loukas, don't you remember me? Loukas looked at him, rubbed his chin and rumbled, "Yes, my boy, I know you from some place." "I am Stavros the husband of Maria, your wife's first cousin." Reminiscences flowed and the efforos smiled warily. Again we had the tremendous luck of finding family in the bureaucracy which provided the infallible "meson". Suffice it to say we paid the tax but it was definitely a "family rate".

Without Loukas things could rapidly spin out of control. One time I needed a small VW van to transport students to different athletic events. One of our bus contractors heard that we were looking to purchase a van and he offered to sell us one. We agreed on a price and he said that all we had to do was go down to the motor vehicle office, pay for some stamps and he would then sign the car over to me. Getting something, anything done in one day with the bureaucracy seemed a stretch to me. But the Sotiris was a bus contractor, a Greek who knew the system. He informed me that at some point in his career he had been employed at the office we were going to. We agreed to meet on a particular day and presented ourselves to the clerk responsible for supervising auto sales.

The office had the usual pale green walls, naked light bulbs hanging from the ceiling and the funky smell of burning cigarettes and greek coffee on the boil. We submitted the papers and the clerk held up one of our papers if it had been used to wipe a baby's bottom. "What is this?" He asked with great suspicion. "It is a power of attorney that allows me to act on behalf of the school. With this document I can sell or buy property and legally act on behalf of the school that I represent." He pounced with cunning and suspicion oozing from every pore, "But where does it say that you can purchase a red, VW van?" He wouldn't hear of our protestations that it gave me generic powers to purchase a range of things on behalf of the school. He insisted that it had to specifically state that it allowed me to purchase a red, VW van.

Muttering we left the office and I explained to Sotiris that I would contact the owners of the school in Switzerland and have them send down permission to purchase a red, VW van. That took ten days to get everything set. We returned to the genetleman at the motor vehicle office and again with suspicion he viewed our documents and once more he pounced. Looking at the power of attorney he said, "Who is Paul Zazzaro?" I explained that he was the business manager of the organization that I worked for and he was the legal representative of the company. "Yes, but how do we know that?" He smiled triumphantly! Rising to his full height and powers he said, "We must have confirmation of who you say he is!" No amount of arguing by Sotiris or me helped. If anything it caused the clerk to dig his heels in further. At this point the Sotiris was apoplectic, but I looked upon it as an existential farce. It took another two weeks before we got the verification from the Greek Embassy in Zurich that Mr. Zazzaro was who he said he was. In the meantime Sotiris and I had exchanged money with the agreement that he would continue to keep the van under his name and covered by his insurance until we were finally able to find our way out of the rabbit hole.

With paper in hand certifying that Mr. Zazzaro was who he claimed to be we returned to the Motor Vehicle office. This paper was from the Greek Embassy in Zurich with the proper Greek stamps and signatures. The clerk took it from us and shrieked, "What is this? What is this?" We explained it was the paper that he had asked for certifying that Mr. Zazarro was who he claimed to be. Cunningly he asked, "And what language is this?" We explained that it was written by the Greek Embassy in Zurich in French which is considered the language of diplomacy. "No, no, no it must be written in Greek! That is the language we speak in Greece!" Stunned I was now obliged to have the letter from the Greek Embassy in Zurich, translated into Greek. This took another two weeks and when I received the translation I called Sortiris and we agreed to meet again at the Motor Vehicle office. On the day I arrived early in time to hear the director say, "Oh, we have too many people out with the flu today. We won't be transferring any cars." By this time I thought the whole situation was absurd and I walked out in time to meet Sotiris and tell him what I had heard. "Impossible!" he screamed. He dragged me by the arm and nearly carried me to the office of the director which he threw open and in an unrelenting stream of Greek poured out his anguish and anger. "How could it be possible that it has taken us almost two months to transfer title of an automobile where in any civilized country it is done in hours not weeks." "I have lived abroad", he shouted. I know how these things should be done. This man is a foreigner and you have put him through this charade. How can we be considered a civilize country?" I was getting very nervous because the director was in uniform and I suspected he was a security police officer. I had visions of us being hauled off to jail for insulting the national honor. The officer surprised me and said to the clerks standing in the doorway. "Transfer title for the gentlemen's car." and he gently led us out of the office. I had witnessed outbursts like Sotiris at the Electricity Office, the Tax Office and the Post Office. Sometimes people became so angry and frustrated that they snapped. Resolution was not always as peaceful as ours had been.

THE FAMILY

EVANGELIA AND STAMMATIS TANGAS

AFTER THE HOUSE WAS COMPLETED, our second set of neighbors, the Tangas, assumed responsibility for us because we were foreigners and obviously could not take care of ourselves. The family consisted of four brothers. Two of them, Stamatis and Apostoli, were in business together. They were plumbers, iron mongers and jacks of all trades as you must be when you live in the country. It was a very handy arrangement and we learned at first hand about the tendency of Greeks to add foreigners to their large extended family on the basis of you can never tell when we might need these people. Once you are drawn into the family circle you are the recipient of their tremendous largess: meals were cooked for us, repairs made on the house and the plumbing and never a drachma changed hands. They were happy and honored by the pleasure of our company because we were foreigners and very "learned". As a "kathyitis" (Professor) I had a very high standing. Our Greek improved as we sat at their table set outside under the olive trees. We were never less than ten or twelve people and they loved to pile our plates high with tasty cheese pies, homemade bread baked in the outdoor beehive shaped ovens. Chicken, fish, lamb, fresh vegetables, vast quantities of homemade retsina, watermelons, fresh (goat's cheese) mezithra cheese were disposed of with noisy exuberance.

At the table we learned about the war and how they liked the Italians but they did not care for the Germans. When the Germans were around there was always trouble and someone was bound to die. The Italians, however, liked children and played guitars and shared some of their spoils with the populace as they plundered their flour, olive oil and fresh produce. But the Italians were human and in the end oppressed when Italy capitulated to the allies. Some Italians were hidden in Greek homes until the end of the war.

We learned about the Civil War from the anti-Communist side. In all of these tales one was left with sense of good people just trying to stay alive and escape from the death and misfortune that surrounded them. They celebrated life with exuberance and each moment was a special event when you were with them. We became part of their mythology: "Do you remember the time when Mr. George danced on the table and Mrs. Suzanne danced the Tsiftitelli with the women? Poh, Poh." But their universe was dark and fearful. There was Smyrna, Turkey's ethnic cleansing of the Greek population seared into everyone's mind after the First World War, crushing poverty, the Second World War and the bloody Civil War in which Greeks killed each other in greater numbers than even the hated Germans. Politicians regularly betrayed them and not even the monarchy provided any stability. The monarchy was deposed three times in the twentieth century. It seemed to us that the only stable factor in Greek History was instability and violent change. Not even the earth remained stable under the tread of the Greek. The country was subject to violent earthquakes and disastrous forest fires which we had experienced at first hand. Through it all the enduring lesson seemed to be that the family was what counted most. Your enduring loyalty was to family and friends, your village or your region and then after that the nation, and whatever else was out there. The stabilizing factors in the Greek world were: family and friends. The family from time immemorial had been the only unit that had defied the pressures and strains of the outside world and had given the Greek some semblance of stability. The family provided food, clothing and shelter to the children until they are ready to marry and leave the house. And very often they did not go far because an apartment had been prepared in the same house for the children. It wasn't considered appropriate for a young woman or man to leave the family home and live on their own. If it was done the parents would try to cover it up.

The bond between mother and son was oedipal and made it very difficult for the daughter- in- law to live a separate life. Sunday dinner was a tradition in many families where the married children came round to the parents to eat. It appeared that no woman was suitable for the son. There was a story going around years ago that Jesus Christ in fact was Greek not Jewish and the proof rests on the fact that, he lived at home until he was 30, went into the family business, his mother thought that he was god and he thought that she was a virgin. Sons are valued and the women have to make do with being considered less valued. When my daughter was born many of our Greek friends said: "Ah, that is nice….., a girl. Don't worry the next one will be a boy!".

Interestingly enough, the women because they had to work doubly hard for affection, recognition and success were often light years more suited to the rough and tumble of life. Many of my Greek friends lived lives that I first thought were suffocating. You rarely had private space because you were always involved with the family. When we built our house in Evia the property that we chose was in a forested area at a distance from the town. Our Greek friends were horrified. How can you live out there all by yourselves in the forest? What will you do? This need for company was demonstrated in a number of ways: When we went to an empty beach and picked out a spot if a Greek family arrived they would come and sit down right next to us even if they had two miles of beach on which to spread out. Of course, they would offer to share their meal with us and quiz us to learn all about us. Another example was Stamatis and Evangelia's concern when I had to go to Athens and leave my wife for the day. They would offer to send Yiaya to stay with her so that she would not be lonely. We always graciously declined.

Children were part of the family and as a result were never left at home. They were always brought to the taverna to eat with the grown ups and allowed to run around visiting other diners. Children were a passport in Greece. They were loved and coddled and cared for even by strangers. Their preciousness was understood and as a result every Greek was a 'Catcher in the Rye'. In England they'll make a great fuss over dogs but children are expected to remain at home! Another advantage to have a large extended network of friends is the Greek passion for networking. As I have pointed out it pays to know a range of people to get things done. If you want to buy a car, petition a Minister, select a school, find an electrician all of this requires introductions from friends so that the job is done correctly and you do not get cheated.

Friends are expected to keep in touch and not just by phone. You visit each other, go on holidays together and meet for dinner on a regular basis. Friends come to your house when you celebrate the Saint's Day that coincides with your name. Birthdays are not celebrated per se. Friends even help you pass exams. Cheating was not considered wrong because the educational system supported it in many ways by being harsh with very exacting standards. As a result cheating was not considered unethical. It was viewed as just a means of beating an unfair system. Greeks would always try to find out who you are and where you arer from to see if there is a connection that can bring you into their orbit. In Greece 'networking was a long time in place before it was defined in the U.S.

Stamatis offered us friendship because that was the type of person that he was, but he also believed that you could never have too many friends. You just never knew when you might need help. As a result of the friendship they offered their services and would never expect money. Years later they came to us for help and we were able to give advice and help with the children's education.

FRIENDSHIP

MY FRIENDSHIP WITH THE FAMILIES OF STAMATIS AND LOUKAS provided us with a safety net in dealing with the vagaries of Greek life at that time. My introduction to Greek hospitality and friendship came when I was teaching at the New School for Social Research in New York. We had a number of Greek students who were studying English and they were the friendliest and most outgoing. I would invite my class to my home at the beginning of the semester to get to know them better. We would ask them to bring a dish and music that was representative of their country. The Greek students were always quick to bring tons of food and wine and then to invite us back to their homes or extend an invitation to go to Greek Town for dinner and dancing.

Learning their stories gave us insight into importance of family and their work ethic. In many instances the father was the first to come over to the U.S. and then the wife and the family. They would all work and raise enough capital to borrow money to open a small business. It used to be that the son did not marry until the sister was provided with a dowry and married. Sometimes this required the son to work in a foreign country or work as a seaman to raise money for the dowry.

To understand the Greek you must understand that the Greek universe centers around the family, friends of the family and the region that they came from. The Greek owes allegiance to family and friends, the national state is not of importance and to be viewed with suspicion. How else is it that the vast majority of people avoid paying taxes? What has the government ever tried to do for me? It comes down to who can you trust. The Greek Universe is fraught with catastrophe and upheaval from 1453 the fall of Constantinople to 1821 Greece except for the Ionian Islands was part of the Ottoman Empire. In 1821 to 1832 the Greek War of Independence liberated part of modern Greece. Greece was placed under the protection of Britain, France and Russia. In 1864 a Danish king is crowned George I. In 1912-1913 territories are added which round out the lands of modern Greece. In 1922 there is a disastrous military defeat in Asia Minor and the Greek forces withdraw. In 1923 the Treaty of Lausanne cedes all territory in Asia Minor to Turkey and there is a huge influx of Greek refugees in exchange of ethnic minorities between Greece and Turkey. From 1936 to 1941 Greece is under The dictatorial regime of General Ioannis Metaxas. In 1941 the Nazis invade and occupy Greece till 1944. From 1946 till 1949 there is Civil War between the communists and the Government. From 1967 to 1974 a military junta takes over. In 1974 the junta falls, democratic institutions are restored and the monarchy is abolished. Cyprus is invaded by Turkey and the island is partitioned.

I have written about Loukas and Tassoula and how they could never do enough for us and never ask for anything in return. When my parents came to visit, we stayed at their country home because ours had not yet been completed. Their friendship and generosity went on for years long after their daughter, Katerina, had left the college and went on to the university. One afternoon I received a call from Tassia. Loukas had been taken to the hospital with a heart attack. To complicate matters it happened when they were in the country and baby sitting the daughter's German shepherd. The shepherd was a scary monster and not at all friendly. As long as the family was around he was fairly docile, but without them he would bare his fangs and look at you like you were the last pork chop on the plate, in short he was an excellent guard dog with a killer instinct.

All of these years the family had never asked me for anything. This was my moment. I told Tassoula that I would drive up to the country and pick up the dog and keep him at my house where I had a large backyard. I was in the middle of a meeting when the call came in. I excused myself, told my secretary that I was gone for the day. It was a three hour drive to the country house. I arrived at about six in the evening after tearing up mountain roads, dodging potholes and madly driven trucks and tractors. I stopped at the local taverna for a cup of coffee and told the owner that I was there to pick up Tassoula's dog. "Po, po, po," he said. "You've come for the killer...be careful my friend." With a racing heart I drove up to the house and figured the best thing to do was open the passenger side door and then open the garden gate hoping that the "Killer" would get into the car. I had some dog treats with me to lure him in.   To my surprise and relief he jumped in without a snarl, and ate the treats. I drove home with his head companionably resting on my shoulder all the way back. We kept the dog for a week and he got along with our dogs and never once menaced anyone who came to the house. I had finally been able to, in a small way, act as a friend to my friends.

The eighties and the nineties were years of change in Greece and in my personal life. The political scene did not show much change. Predominantly two major parties right and left governed by two political families. In 1981 Greece joined the Common Market. The Berlin Wall came down and there was Glasnost. But Greece still maintained one of the only Communist Parties in Europe. The drachma climbed from 30 drachmas to the dollar to ninety. Television went from two channels to ten. There were more imported products on the shelves and supermarkets arrived to push out the small shop keeper. And many of the Greek brands of products disappeared. There were around 20 daily newspapers but an unprecedented 42 Sports news papers, which underlines the Greek passion for football.

In my personal life, Suzanne and I separated in 1981 and divorced in 1985. I married again in 1986 to my present wife,

Jane.   In 1984 I became headmaster of an international school in Athens, TASIS.   It was a private school under the direction of an amazing American woman Mary Crist Fleming who had established schools in England and Switzerland and for a brief period in Cyprus and France.   Larger than life she was an outstanding educator who established centers of learning that allowed students to flourish in multicultural environments.   She was extremely demanding in her expectations but lots of fun to work with.   I took over the school after my friend was forced to resign over the issue involving the Cypriot teacher and the Model United Nations which was described earlier.

I was in Boston at the time working on an Ed.D. in educational administration when I got a call to act as an advisor to the school. They thought my connections with the ministry would be of help during this time of crisis.   Unfortunately the Ministry was adamant and my friend was forced to leave.   When I joined the school I found a dedicated faculty, supportive parents and students.   Like Lake Woebegone: at TASIS "all the women are strong, all the men are good looking, and all the children are above average".   I had a contact in the newspaper business who knew a minister who was influential in the Ministry of Education.   My question to my contact was, "Do they intend to close the school?"   I didn't want to assume the captaincy of the Titanic mid-Atlantic.   The answer came back that there was no interest in closing the school but "be careful".

The school offered a curriculum that allowed students to pre-pare for entrance to either American or British Colleges.   We were "careful" and avoided major incidents but there were adventures as there always was in Greece.   I had a business manager who decided unbeknownst to me to "postpone" paying social security taxes so that we would look healthier to our TASIS administrators.   One morning he informed me that we had a court appointment to settle some financial problems.   On the appointed day we arrived in court with our lawyer and I was told when to stand up and declare my presence. I understood very little of the proceedings. I was fairly fluent in Greek at the time, however, I had little understanding of the legalese.

After the court session was over I invited my colleagues to go to a café where they could explain what the proceedings had been all about. It was then that I learned we had been brought to court for non payment of social security. The business manager said, "It was basically what I expected." "Yes", nodded my lawyer sagely, "a ten year sentence." "What?" I croaked. They were quick to assure me that in Greek jurisprudence, being sentenced like that was just an incentive to paying the fines. If it had been more than ten years, then I would have had to serve time. The next day I changed the locks on the business office and appointed a new business manager who served me well and loyally and to this day still works at the school.

In 1996 my daughter, Alessia, was born and though I had planned on retiring in Greece, I now felt that I wanted to bring her back to America to enjoy the benefits of living in a society that had served me well and provided so many opportunities at home and in Greece. At that time the TASIS organization asked me to find a buyer for the school which I was able to accomplish. We flew home on August 25, 1997, 32 years to the day when I had first arrived in Greece.

Many years have passed but the memories and the friendships are fresh in my mind. There are nights when I still dream of Evia and the house. Though I have returned several times to Greece to see my friends, I have been unable to go back to Evia. I have tried to close that chapter because I know of the many changes that have occurred since I left, but it remains open and in my dreams I return to the house convinced that I did not sell it and it still is mine peopled with the spirits of my friends George, the builder, Stamatis and Evangelia, Loukas and Tassia, Philip and Eda, George and Eleni the taverna owners, and all the friends who helped to make it the final destination of my Greek Odyssey.

EPILOGUE

IT IS 2011 NOW AND GREECE is very much in the news. It requires massive economic assistance from the European Community or its default could cause the collapse of the EU. The nation is under tremendous criticism because it allegedly provided false information to be admitted to the EU in the first place. It stands accused of wasting the money that the EU had given them by patronage for supporters of the various governments and sheer incompetence. Adding to Greece's problems is a top heavy, ineffective bureaucracy unable to collect taxes. The nepotistic political parties stand condemned because they refused to take decisions that would have ameliorated the present economic melt down.

I spent thirty-two years of my life in Greece. I went there to avoid the "predictability" of what my life would have been in the United States: marriage, job, kids and a move to the suburbs. I sought travel and adventure, and Greece provided all of that and more. It provided deep, life long friendships and professional opportunities that allowed me to develop skills in communication and personal growth. I met people who shared different life styles and philosophies that forced me to examine my American drive to climb higher and higher on the professional ladder. Becoming top dog is not necessarily the secret ingredient leading to success and personal happiness. Greece and the Greeks taught me so many valuable life lessons.

Why does this land stand condemned today? David Holdin in his book <u>Greece Without Columns</u>, p. 84, wrote "It is scarcely possible to review the Greek record of internecine warfare, crumbling governments, fissile parties and bickering oppositions, coups, plots, and counter coups, without suspecting that all these things are at least as much an expression of the fundamental character of Greekness as the result of mere historical misfortunes."

I believe that what constitutes the character of a people comes from the geography and history of the land in which they reside. Two thirds of this achingly beautiful country is comprised of mountains and approximately a sixth is comprised of arable lands. Villages located in the mountains were independent principalities like the city states of ancient times. These conditions made Greeks rugged individualists, loyal to family and village. Central authority, the government, was distrusted. When I arrived in Greece in 1965 it was a turbulent political time and I was told that a poll had been taken to determine who was best qualified to address the problems of the country. Three out of four respondents replied "Me!". When a Greek man gets up to dance, traditionally he dances like Zorba, alone.

When the Government came round to tax, these monies brought no benefit to the village. Cheating the tax man just made good sense. Why pay for something that brings you nothing in return? A man was considered 'poniros' clever like a fox who could outwit the taxman. Greek heroes like Odysseus were 'poniros'. To be 'poniros' was a virtue in the eyes of the Greek. Because of the isolation of the villages Greek loyalties were more tribal and familial. First loyalty was to family and friends and then the village. These were the people you could trust and depend on. Time and again I was privy to anecdotes that took place during the German occupation and the brutal civil war where condemned men and women were saved at the last minute because a family member or a fellow villager was able to warn them to escape. The family connections served Loukas and I well when we went to do battle with the taxman. It was family and political connections that got us a substantial reduction.

The individuality of the Greek was revealed to me during the forest fire on Evia when I failed miserably at attempting to form a bucket brigade. I couldn't get the men to pass the bucket. Every time I gave someone the bucket they wouldn't pass it but would run off in a different direction! A former acquaintance who coached the national basketball team for a while said the his greatest difficulty was getting the players to function as a team. Time and again players refused to pass the ball. And then there is the old saying, I believe, attributed to Churchill, "Put two Greeks in a room and they will form three political parties."

Another aspect of the Greek character is his 'philotimou', his pride or honor. Touch a man's 'philotimou' and he can be motivated to do something even against his best interests. I was told this story years ago by a friend who was a witness to this event. A man stopped a cab and asked the cabbie to put a couple of gallon jugs of olive oil in his trunk. The cabbie refused because he knew the oil would inevitably leak and his trunk would be a mess. The man with the oil quoted a saying with a twist, instead of saying "Poor but good." he accused the cabbie of being "Poor but not good." The cabbie's philotomou was tested and he reacted by picking up the jugs of oil and putting them in the trunk as he said to the passenger, "Poor but good".

To read the history of modern Greece from 1821 to the present day is to understand that this young nation, younger that the United States, has lurched from one disaster to the next. Nothing in its history appeared to be stable. There were wars, hostile occupations, coups, counter coups, multiple changes of government, and multiple constitutions. In 1923 there was a forced population exchange which brought to Greece a million Greeks from Anatolia, southern Turkey, where they had resided for centuries. Greece was always surrounded by enemies and at war at different times with Bulgaria, Albania and the former Yugoslavia. In the background there was always the threat of the hereditary enemy Turkey which had occupied Greece for over 500 years. At times not even the earth underneath their feet was stable as earthquakes rocked the land and fires devoured the few remaining forests.

Greece from the outset of its nationhood was always a client state, looking to the major powers of the time: Russia, France, Britain and finally the United States. As a result there was always someone to blame for meddling into their politics and actions. Why did the Greeks chose a foreign king to rule them? Otto Prince of Bavaria in 1832 was invited to rule the land because no Greek would have accepted one of their own to hold this position. Greeks hold a low regard for each other but have the highest opinion of themselves. I remember John from the Queen Frederika telling me never to trust his countrymen. He was, he assured me, the only Greek I could trust.

Yet when you look at the countless Greeks who immigrated to Europe, Australia, Africa and the United States you see the Greek thrive and prosper. He is a model citizen who works within the law and the customs of his adopted country. Abroad he is an astute business man who pays his taxes, establishes an Orthodox church, keeps his family and friends close and ensures that his children learn Greek at home and English at school and absorbs as much education as possible. In the U.S. the accomplishments of the Greek communities are significant rising to prominence in politics the names of John Brademas, John Sarbanes, Michael Dukakis, not to overlook Vice President Spyros Agnew who unfortunately was more 'poniros' then was good for him and led him to succumb to the ancient sin of 'hubris'. Most recently Arianna Stassinopoulos Huffington is a famous Greek-American author and syndicated columnist. The list of successful Greek-Americans goes on.

Today superhighways span the country and villages are not isolated. Traveling from Athens to Delphi or the Peloponnesos used to take hours with an adventure never far away, but now these journeys can be accomplished faster and in safety. The hope for

Greece is in the strength, intelligence and resilience of its people who deserve leaders with vision. Leaders who are not hampered by the feudal traditions of the past. Leaders who will forswear greed, patronage and partisanship and serve the people as stewards of a culture that can be led to escape the bonds of the past and labor to instill discipline and respect not only for the law but for each other. It will take a cultural revolution but they are capable and their time has come.

October 30, 2011: I have just returned from a month long trip to Greece. Previously I ended this narrative on a positive note, but history has made a mockery of my prediction. I was witness to the takeover of Greece by European technocrats to insure that it will eventually meet its obligations to the EU and continue to receive economic support. It was a month of watching politicians behaving badly and the press fueling a twenty four seven feeding frenzy of rumor and invective. Prime Minister Papandreou did his best to negotiate a deal but he had no cards to play. Time had run out for him and the country. Of course, the burden of past mistakes has been placed on the people and new taxes and demands for austerity are theirs to bear. A final observation: A new tax has been imposed by DEH, the national electric company. It is based on the square footage of the home or place of business. This is a one time tax that the government dreamed up to help meet its obligations and ensure that it would, in fact, be collected. If it is not paid then the electricity is cut. But already the citizenry is addressing this by occupying the DEH offices and some municipalities are offering to illegally reconnect homes that have been cut off, plus ça change plus c'est la même chose.

Despite the depressing and often alarming news, friends greeted me warmly and fussed over me. Though everyone was stressed and slightly depressed, hospitality was unbounded and there was the determination that the betrayal by their leaders and the economic chaos would eventually pass. I can make no predictions and I have no idea how things will turn out, but a part of me is forever tied to this beautiful land and her gracious, generous and industrious people. In my heart I know they have the ability and strength to overcome this present chaos. History has not always been kind to the Greeks but they have always managed to rise from the ashes like the mythical phoenix. This passage in their history should be no different. In my own personal history the best half of my life was spent amongst them and I will always be grateful for that honor and privilege.

16194661R00081

Made in the USA
Charleston, SC
09 December 2012